HORIZONS
OF
HOPE

An Autobiography

by

John G. Pribram

Best wishes
Thanks for all your support
John G. Pribram

3/22/06

Printed in the U.S.A.
Holbrook Printing
Tulsa, Oklahoma

Horizons of Hope © 1991 John G. Pribram

For information address:
Horizons of Hope
5397 East 26th Street
Tulsa, Oklahoma 74114-4901
email: jpribram@cox.net

Printed in the United States of America
Cover Portrait - Agnete Pribram - AP Photo

First Edition, 1991
Publisher's-Cataloging in Publication Data

Pribram, John G., 1924 –

HORIZONS OF HOPE is the author's autobiography
p. cm.

1. Pribram, John G., 1924 -   2. World War, 1939-1945 - Europe
3. World War, 1939-1945 - Biography   4. History, Modern - 20th Century
5. Social Science Education

I. Title

1991 923.7   (B)   940.53'092'3   LC: 91-076307
ISBN: 1-880488-08-6   ISBN: 1-880488-09-4

Revised Edition, 2001
ISBN: 097041-X $10.00   LC: 00-093523

Revised Edition, 2006
ISBN: 0970414528 $10.00   Library of Congress Control Number: 06921931

HORIZONS
OF
HOPE

I would like to express my gratitude to my wife Agnete, to Mrs. Norma Jean Lutz, a Tulsa author, and to Mrs. Martha Embry, a Tulsa educator, for all the help and advice I received in writing the story of my life.

For this updated revised edition of "Horizons of Hope" I would like to thank Jarvis Harriman, a Tucson author, and John Robin Allen, professor from the University of Manitoba for their valuable help I receive from them.

A special thanks go to Dr. Ekdahl, Executive Director of Emeritus, Independent Schools Association of the Southwest, for his valuable help in the creation of this third edition of "Horizons of Hope".

This story is dedicated to the next generation. May you have the courage and wisdom to create a hunger-free, greed-free, hate-free and fear-free world.

Preface

By John G. Pribram

My childhood in Czechoslovakia, the escape on a bicycle from the Nazis, the crossing of the ocean during submarine warfare, combat during World War II, and the participation in the Postwar Reconstruction of Europe are some of the experiences I had the opportunity to tell to individuals and to various groups.

In my twenty-five years as an educator and history teacher, I used these personal experiences in my classes. The students gained a better understanding of World War II and of the Postwar Reconstruction of Europe.

I was encouraged by my friends to write about my experiences. It is now half a century ago that World War II started. We won the war and tried to build a world of prosperity and peace.

For forty-five years we lived under the threat of a nuclear war. Now the "Cold War" is finally over, the Super-powers are working things out together, but problems about the economy in both East and West, the Middle East crisis, the global destruction of our environment, and starvation in parts of Africa are still making the headlines.

In America apathy, disappointment with our elected officials, concern about the education of our youth, increase in crime and in homelessness make us believe, that wherever we look, there is lack of faith and hope.

I decided to write my personal story so it would be available to more people. It will give encouragement to those who are determined to build a better world, and it may give faith and hope to those who need it. Thus, it may contribute to the creation of a better world we long to see.

Horizons of Hope
TABLE OF CONTENTS

PART I:
Escape and World War II

Castle - Prague, Czechoslovakia

CHAPTER 1
It Can't Happen Here

It was a warm, sunny day in September 1938. Hundreds of grim-faced citizens stood waiting quietly in Wenceslas Square in Prague, Czechoslovakia. Even the children and babies were quiet, as they seemed to sense the seriousness of the moment.

I was not much more than a child myself at age fourteen. I looked across the square at the statue of King Wenceslas towering unchangeable over the crowd. There stood the National Museum that I'd visited many times. Nearby was the Charles University, the oldest University in Central Europe, where I would be attending school in a few years to study to become a doctor like my uncle.

At least that had been my plan, my dream. But now I stood with friends and neighbors waiting for the news from Munich, where leaders of Great Britain, France, Italy and Hitler's Germany were deciding the fate of the young nation of Czechoslovakia.

All citizens of our country were ready to fight Germany, to defend our country, to give our lives to preserve freedom. Blackouts were a natural thing for us, as we expected German air raids at any time. Shelters were ready in every house, even an evacuation of Prague was planned. Buses were at the Rumanian border, ready to transport Russian troops to help us.

My quiet peaceful life, as I had known it, was hanging in the balance—resting on the decision of a few men at that Munich conference.

I was born in the lovely old city of Prague and lived there during my childhood years. Mine was a very protected life. My parents, Ewald and Marianne Pribram, and my elder brother, Otto, and other family members meant everything to me.

At Christmas we gathered around a huge Christmas tree at the home of my grandparents. My mother had four brothers and one sister. Most of them were married, and they all came with their children for the big celebration. I can still see grandfather lighting the candles on the tree and keeping watch over them with a water bucket nearby.

As a child I was told the Christ child was giving all the gifts. I remember my disappointment at age five when I discovered I had received a gift from my uncle. I felt my mother had lied to me. However, she explained that Jesus **was** actually working through people, and the family was fulfilling His wishes. I accepted that explanation.

We lived in a four bedroom apartment with a living room, dining room, and a study with a huge library for Father and a piano for Mother. Otto had his own study, and the bedroom, that he and I shared during the night was my study and playroom during the day. Our home was filled with plants and flowers since my mother loved them. On the walls were many pictures of the city of Prague.

The ladies who served as our maid and cook were sisters. They lived with us and looked after us. Once a week their aunt came to do the laundry for us. They were kind, friendly ladies.

My father was a lawyer for an important Czech corporation and made a comfortable living. On weekends we would take long walks to the old part of Prague to explore the Old City and appreciate our heritage.

Mother and Father were devoted to my brother Otto and me. Mother had an ear for foreign languages and helped us to learn French and English. She also made it her priority to oversee our schoolwork in Czech and German. She played the piano and insisted that my brother and I take lessons. She was proud of her many pastry recipes and could have prepared a different dessert daily for a month and a half.

Father taught me to play chess. I can remember how proud I was when, after a visit to Austria, where a Hungarian chess champion taught me some special moves, I actually beat my father!

During summer holidays we traveled to different European countries. When I was five, my parents took me skiing in the nearby mountains. They took me to the top of a hill and asked me to slide down and then walk up again. At the end of the day, I was black and blue from numerous falls. For several years after that I refused to go skiing.

One summer, I was permitted to join my father in climbing one of Austria's highest mountains, the Gross-Venediger. To cross a glacier, we had a guide and used ropes and icepicks. Reaching the summit and viewing the vast expanse of snow-covered Alps surrounding us was a magnificent experience.

Another summer we went to Yugoslavia. I discovered their language was similar to ours, and I could easily talk to the natives. We visited the beautiful waterfalls at Plitvice. We went fishing and returned to our hotel with crabs to cook for our dinner. However, when I saw these eyes looking at me, I refused to join my parents in the meal.

My parents believed that education was not done just in a classroom but involved all of life. This concept would follow me throughout my life.

The pleasant experience of those early years were marred only by the death of my uncle who drowned, followed by the death of grandfather. This was the first time I faced death. I knew I would never see them again, but they would live in my memory forever.

When grandfather was seventy years old, all the children and grandchildren produced a play for him. An uncle who was a playwright wrote the play. I was only five at the time and excited to be included. I played the role of a waiter. Grandfather was so moved by the celebration, he gave gifts to each of us. I still have the pair of opera glasses I received on that memorable day.

After grandfather died, my grandmother became even more devoted to her family. Once a year she arrived from her home in Vienna to stay with us. It was the highlight of the year for Otto and me. Grandmother was a sensitive lady who enjoyed talking to us, reading stories to us, and even playing games with us.

When the Nazis occupied Austria, she went to Belgium to live with one of her children. There she remained in hiding throughout the German occupation. Following the war she finally managed to join her family in United States and lived to be ninety years old. Grandmother was truly a selfless person who wrote encouraging letters when needed and whose home and heart were always open to me. I learned much from her life.

My family instilled in me a love and respect for my homeland. Ours was still a young democratic nation in 1938. Czechoslovakia was formed by the uniting of the Czechs and Slovaks in 1918 under the leadership of Thomas G. Masaryk, the first President of Czechoslovakia. Masaryk had spent most of his life preparing for the independence of his country and helped to draft the first Czechoslovak Constitution, which was modeled after the American Constitution. A healthy administration made Czechoslovakia one of the most stable and prosperous democracies in Central Europe.

The country, approximately the size of New York State, is rich in agricultural and mineral resources and is highly developed industrially. The people are hardworking, industrious and freedom loving.

It was into this prosperous and peaceful time that I was born in 1924. Now I stood among the pensive, milling crowd awaiting the news. News that would change our lives forever.

We were horrified when we learned that our allies, France and Great Britain had let us down. Russia stood ready to help us, but the great nations of Europe asked us for a greater sacrifice:

"Save the peace, give Hitler the German-speaking part of Czechoslovakia, the Sudetenland, give him your fortifications, demobilize your armies. We want peace. Hitler promised peace. He is not going to do anything to you." This was known as the Munich Pact of 1938 or more correctly "Appeasement at any Price."

The atmosphere of the crowd in the square immediately turned to despair. Our country had been betrayed. We had sided with the great democracies, and they had sold us out. I can remember a great feeling of loss. None of us believed that Hitler would keep his word, for if he took part of the country now, eventually, he would take it all.

The desire of the crowd was for the Red Army to help, but it was too late. However, in 1945, Czechoslovakia remembered vividly the shock of the Munich Pact, and they turned to the Soviet Union. That is why it became a communist country—this time betrayed by the promises of the East. It would not be until the "Velvet" Revolution of 1989 that Czechoslovakia would be free again.

In 1938, Czechoslovakia surrendered the Sudetenland, but that act did not bring peace. The fortifications were taken without a fight. The Nazis agreed later that it would have been difficult to take the country by fighting. My country suffered terribly. The days of supreme patriotism were followed by sadness and tears.

My plans to finish my high school education in Prague and then attend the famous Charles University were suddenly dashed into nothing.

My parents began to think seriously of sending me away to a safer place. The schools had become overcrowded by refugees from the Sudetenland. Everyone doubted that Hitler would be satisfied with that portion of the country. It seemed only a matter of time before the Nazis would move further into Czechoslovakia. Then what would be my chances of gaining an education?

So it was decided that I would leave my beloved family and go to live with my mother's brother in Belgium. I was to continue my high school education at the Institut de Gand, a private French-speaking school. Belgium was a neutral country, so I would be able to come home for the holidays.

Otto had already been sent to America. He had stood ready to join the Czech Army, but after the Munich Pact he was deeply disappointed. He was invited by my father's brother Karl and his wife Edith to come to the States. There he attended Swarthmore College and later studied at Columbia University.

The company where my father had worked as a lawyer was headquarters for large mines and glass factories in the Sudetenland. Once that area was taken by the Nazis, my father's job was non-existent because the firm had to close. This, of course, added to our shock and concern for the future.

Until 1938, I had never thought much about the world, and even when Hitler took over Germany, I was convinced he would only rule Germans. Now I was thrust from the familiar surroundings that I had known so well. Away from my family who loved me dearly. It was one of the most difficult moments of my life.

My mind was filled with gnawing questions of, would I ever see my family again? Would I ever go home again? Would I one day follow in the footsteps of my uncle and other relatives and become a doctor? Or was I to leave the past forever behind me?

I was filled with fear and misgivings as I boarded the train from Prague crossing Germany. Five others joined my compartment in Germany. At the German-Belgian border, the train stopped. Our passports were examined by border guards. The German SS arrived on the scene, pointing their pistols at everyone. I was a citizen of Czechoslovakia and was allowed to go on. But my five companions were forced to leave the train. Only God knows what happened to them.

In Belgium, I got a brief taste of new hope. I made many new friends in the school and enjoyed living with my uncle Adolphe and aunt Christa Furth. I tried to forget what was happening in the world and to concentrate on my new life.

However, three months after my arrival, we received word that Hitler had invited Dr. Hacha, the new President of Czechoslovakia, to Berlin. There, Hitler gave him an ultimatum: to surrender his country peacefully, or Prague, the capital, would be destroyed by bombs and the country would be taken by force. In the face of this pressure, Dr. Hacha suffered a heart attack. As soon as he recovered sufficiently, he was forced to sign the document of surrender.

By taking Czechoslovakia, Hitler broke his promise to limit his conquest to German-speaking people only. Nazi soldiers took over the country, met with little resistance. As the first tanks rolled into the city of Prague, the drivers raided the bakeries, only to find that the Czechs had added ample doses of laxatives to the goodies!

My parents experienced three months of Nazi occupation in Prague. It was an extremely difficult time. My mother worried whether she would ever see her sons again. Some of my parents' friends were questioned by Nazis because of "disloyalty" to the Third Reich. Some ended up in prison, other in concentration camps.

This finally became unbearable for my parents, and they decided to obtain a visitor's permit and join me in Belgium for the summer. Although their future plans were indefinite, they left our apartment virtually as it was. They hoped Belgium would remain neutral in this struggle and soon we would all return home. They also urged my uncle, a well-known physician to come with them, he refused, not wanting to desert his patients. Later he was taken to a concentration camp where he died.

In September 1939, after negotiating a Non-Aggression Pact with the Soviet Union, Hitler invaded Poland. The Soviet Union signed this pact with Germany in order to take part of Poland and later part of Finland.

As these events unfolded, we became increasingly concerned about the future. We surmised that where Hitler did not succeed, Stalin would. Hitler's dictatorship, once broken, would be replaced by Stalin's dictatorship. My parents stayed on in Belgium.

France and Great Britain had aligned themselves with Poland, declaring war on Nazi Germany, thus officially starting the European part of World War II.

There were strong defenses between France and Germany, the Maginot Line and the Siegfried Line, keeping the war at a standstill for a number of months. In the spring of 1940, Hitler invaded Denmark, and then Norway. The Norwegians, backed by the British, put up fierce resistance, but Hitler was successful in taking the country.

Hitler had promised never to attack Belgium, because it was a neutral country, just as he had promised never to attack Czechoslovakia.

On May 10, 1940, the unexpected happened! At five o'clock in the morning, I was awakened by explosions. I jumped to the window. There were planes in the sky, bombing the city of Ghent.

Experiencing a bombing is akin to facing a hurricane or tornado. The initial concern, worry and fear of not surviving is at last replaced with sighs of relief at having lived through it. Our home was spared, but all around there was unbelievable destruction.

I knew the war had come to where I was, and there would be much suffering and endless cruelties.

That first morning I went to school as though nothing had happened. However, the headmaster greeted us sadly and sent us home. The danger of bombardments was too great to risk the lives of children assembled by the hundreds in school buildings.

The headmaster often complained about our lack of discipline. I shall never forget the day he said to us, "In my day, we did not have much discipline, but then during World War I the Germans came and occupied our country. We started to appreciate what freedom really was. I hope this will never happen to you. Sometimes when you do not behave well, I think you may need to experience a German occupation." Little did we know that was really going to happen?

At first I did not realize what the German invasion of Belgium would mean. When I left school, I ran to play a game of tennis. But that afternoon, we saw a plane flying over the city. There had been no air raid warning, so we tried to identify the allied plane. To our surprise, the plane dropped bombs, and we hurriedly took refuge in a shelter.

Many buildings in Ghent had two and three stories *underground*. During air raids the plan was to go as low as possible. As we huddled in that shelter, everything seemed to change. Strangers became friends. We were all afraid of destruction and death, and we had one common objective—survival.

The next day important trains were passing through the city and heavy bombardments made us again seek refuge in the shelters. Near the station where I lived, houses trembled and I expected them to fall. A well-known restaurant where I had eaten several times was hit and totally destroyed.

In the afternoon the mood changed to that of excitement. Allied troops were passing through the city! We were in the streets welcoming the French and English soldiers. We gave them cigarettes, candies and whatever we could find. Morale was high. We were going to win the war!

But five days later, the Nazis were penetrating Belgium and approaching our city. The situation seemed too dangerous to remain in that country. The Belgian government ordered all men from sixteen to forty-five years of age to evacuate the city and move to France as quickly as possible. Of course, only those on bicycles or cars could escape successfully.

My parents and I held a "council of war." We decided it would be better for me to follow the appeal of the Belgian government and to jump on my bicycle and escape as quickly as possible. Mother and father said they would see what they could do and how they could escape. At some later date we would surely find each other again. After all, uncle Karl lived in Washington, D.C., and Otto was studying in the States. We exchanged many addresses so we could communicate through other family members.

It was even more difficult to leave Mother and Father the second time. Words cannot express the deep emotions filling my heart. We had developed an even closer unity as a family in Belgium, yet the war forced us to give it up and once again I bid my parents farewell and fled for my life on a bicycle into an unknown future. Hope hung on a slender thread.

Sometimes I have wondered why people cling to the belief of "it can't happen here; it can't happen to us." Later I realized we were basically a non-involved individualistic society. As long as Hitler threatened some of our neighbors, took the Saar and Austria, we rationalized that it was because they were German-speaking countries. Once he took Czechoslovakia, we blamed France and Great Britain for not helping us. Hitler continued his conquest by taking Poland, Norway, Denmark, Holland, Belgium and France.

Unless democracies stand up together and fight for what they believe is right, one by one they could lose their freedom and suffer the same fate as Czechoslovakia. It was first taken by Hitler's National Socialism and ten years later by Stalin's Communism.

CHAPTER 2
Escape To France

I left Ghent on my bicycle—one that had come with me from Czechoslovakia. It was nothing like the lightweight bicycles of today, but was heavy and solid.

We agreed that my parents would try to leave any way they could, and at a later date we would find each other in France. I had no choice but to leave, because the Belgian government ordered all young men to escape as quickly as possible—perhaps later we would be trained and regrouped to fight the Nazis. My parents were too old for this type of warfare.

I took some necessary clothing, stamps from my stamp collection, a few souvenir gold pieces, and by four o'clock in the afternoon of May 15th, I jumped on the bike and was off. Passing the railroad station, an air raid alert and a bombing by German planes slowed me down. Another alert near the airport forced me to throw my bicycle down and take refuge in a ditch. There I met a Belgian student who was also trying to escape. We decided to travel together. By nightfall we joined forty other students. However, the next day, during another air raid, we lost the forty students and so just the two of us carried on.

A terrifying incident occurred when we came to a Belgian town very near the French border. Suddenly the sirens sounded. Again, I left my bicycle in the middle of the road and hurled myself into a ditch. It was almost too late. The enemy had begun the bombardments of the town.

I heard shots of anti-aircraft guns. The droning of the planes was dreadful. The refugees crowded in the ditches, children cried, women fainted. But then the sound of terrific explosions soon drowned out the noise of planes. Buildings fell down, fires broke out. The bombing became more intense. I dared not look up at the "Stukas," that flew lower and lower, trying to intercept the flight of thousands of refugees, and without pity, dropped bombs on us.

When a bomb dug an enormous hole a few steps from us, stones and debris were hurled in our direction. The panic in the crowd was terrible. When the all-clear rang, we were dumbfounded and hardly dared to breathe with relief.

I tried to find my possessions. I was fortunate to find my bicycle and knapsack. Others had their bicycles smashed by bombs, or they could not find them at all. Many had to continue their flight on foot.

When I put the knapsack on my back, ready to start again, I noticed one wheel was damaged. But I had no tools with me and of course there was no place to buy them. I tried to fix the bicycle, but my efforts were in vain. I tried to get help from other bicycle riders, but some were so frightened by the bombings and the hardship of their flight, they thought only of themselves and did not want to stop and help. Others wanted to help but had no tools.

While I waited for help, a sad procession of refugees passed by. Some were lucky enough to ride in cars or on a bicycle, but there were also old women on foot, dragging or pushing carts overloaded with children, linen, clothing and cooking utensils. They moved forward at an alarmingly slow pace. Many would learn later that their escape was to no avail when Hitler occupied France as well. Some would return to their homes, and a few would be able to leave Europe altogether.

Years later I would think back and marvel that my young Belgian friend waited patiently with me when he could very well have hurried on his way. When I was on the point of giving up and continuing my flight on foot, without any hope of ever escaping the German invaders, a kind fellow helped me repair the damages and we went on.

Soon it became dark. We were thankful to find a haystack for shelter. Of course, we had no food for supper. During the night I heard the roaring of planes, but nevertheless, I tried to sleep and forget the war with all its distress.

Fortunately, my Belgian friend and I passed through towns either before they were bombed or immediately afterwards. At the end of each day, we were hungry and needed shelter for the night but had very little money. We stopped in the villages. When we knocked at the door of a baker he took us in, we knew we would have bread to eat the next day. When a butcher took us in, we would even have meat. We certainly appreciated the French hospitality. They demonstrated a genuine caring and wanted to help us any way they could.

It was a ten-day escape, moving as quickly as possible during the day, and resting as much as possible at night. After about 350 miles we reached Angers, in the center of France. The roads were crowded with people. The French authorities opened up refugee camps and were speeding up our escape by putting the refugees into trains and sending them to the southern part of France.

I was on such a train for over 48 hours. In a boxcar used for eight horses or cattle, more than forty human beings were pressed against each other with no food or drink for most of the journey. This was the first time I experienced how people react under stress. At one station, the Red Cross passed out sandwiches. Some of the refugees acted like hungry animals, trying to get as much as possible. Others preferred to go hungry and not fight their fellowmen.

The journey ended in Lunel, near Montpellier in southern France. We were put into refugee camps where we could recover from the strains of the journey. Unfortunately, my Belgian companion and I were separated when he was sent to a different camp. I do not know what became of him, but I was always grateful we could share the bicycle escape together.

Life in a refugee camp was uneventful and dull. For a sixteen-year-old boy there was nothing for me to do but listen to news of the day, eat inadequate food, and hope for letters from my family.

Emotionally, it was an extremely difficult time. Insecurity and uncertainty are paralyzing forces. Questions nagged at me. Would there be enough food? Would the French keep us in refugee camps? Would the Germans overtake all of France? Were my parents safe? Would I ever hear from them again? Would I remain a refugee forever?

After a few days in the camp, three Belgian married men and I were assigned to an empty flat in one of the poorest sections of the town. We were given blankets on which to sleep, since there were no beds. There were no restrooms, so we used the public facilities of the city.

My Belgian friends showed more initiative than I. Soon they found some hay and put it into sacks for mattresses. We bought vegetables, especially potatoes, and made soup. We acquired a radio and were able to listen to the news. The British talked of their victories, the Germans talked of theirs. It was difficult to know what was going on—but it looked as though the Allies were losing the war.

Then one day France surrendered. The entire population of Lunel assembled in the marketplace in front of City Hall. Over a loud speaker, the new French leader, General Pétain, explained the terms of the surrender. He called for patience and courage. One part of France—the southern part where I was—would remain free. The "Marseillaise," the French National Anthem was played. We listened and people wept. France, the great nation that had produced Napoleon, that had won World War I, was defeated. Hitler was entering Paris. This was the darkest day in its history.

The moment paralleled the day a few years earlier when I stood in Wenceslas Square and heard the news that my country was being taken.

One Sunday I decided to attend church. While I was there, the Protestant clergyman noticed me and invited me to his home for dinner. Later he introduced me to a French family, the Ameyes, who in turn invited me to their home for dinner. I had been subsisting many days on a less than adequate diet. Good food was so rare to me that after dining with them, I became very sick. My new

French friends felt responsible for me, and they invited me to stay. They called a doctor who took care of me.

The Ameyes were respected citizens who owned a clothing store. They were warmhearted people, true patriots with a concern for their fellowman and a love for their country. They had two sons who were still in high school, Jacques and Pierre. One was two years older, the other two years younger than I. They had many friends and included me in their various activities.

Soon I was enjoying this French home and was treated like a member of their family. I attended the French school with Jacques and Pierre and met their friends. Activities of volleyball and studies replaced the boredom of being a refugee.

The Ameyes had a cottage on the Mediterranean. There we spent weekends and holidays, and I was able to go swimming and to relax. Monsieur Ameye had vineyards, and often we would go to pick grapes. The family enjoyed showing me the historical monuments and buildings in the area. From a straw bed in a cheap room, this was a tremendous improvement in my life.

Of course, I was constantly worried about my parents. I had received no news for weeks. One day a letter arrived with what looked like my father's handwriting. But when I opened it, it was from uncle Karl in America informing me about the fate of my parents. They had tried to escape from Belgium. Crossing a river in a boat, they were drowned. My mother's body was found, but the search for my father had been to no avail.

This news was a tremendous shock. My entire life had been centered around my parents. Now I was totally alone. I felt lonely and scared. I thought many times that perhaps I should have stayed with them, but they had insisted on my escape. In a way, I felt a measure of relief for them. They were older, and the life of a refugee is a hard one. Passing on at this time might have been the best.

I had been brought up as a Protestant. However, my religion had not meant a great deal to me until I survived the first bombing. Somehow at that moment, I felt God's protection over me. I felt overwhelmed by God's amazing care for a person like me. I was filled with gratitude that God had provided a home for me. I was thankful that I was settled in a home before I received the news that my parents had died.

Letters from Otto and uncle Karl in America urged me to join them immediately. It was not an easy decision. The French family had provided a home for me. They had sent me to the Collège de Lunel (a French high school), and I made many new friends. Academically I quickly adjusted and performed well. Everything seemed to be all right.

I also knew that Hitler was on the move and would, no doubt, eventually take all of France. I had already lost my family and my country. Why live in this type of insecurity forever? I decided to accept my uncle Karl's invitation. He had been in America for many years, and I did not really know him. Once he and aunt Edith had visited us in Prague, but I was very young.

As for America, I knew very little about the country, except that they drank milk instead of wine and that everyone had a lot of money. But I was faced with the choice of a life under German occupation or a future in a free country.

First, I had to obtain a permit to enter the United States. This was easy because of my American family, but I had to travel to Marseilles and wait for hours in front of the American consulate where hundreds and even thousands of people were trying to get entry visas to the United States. Only a few were admitted to the consulate, but even fewer got their permits to enter the country.

As soon as I had this precious paper, I had to obtain a permit to leave France. This took several additional weeks. Finally I decided to take a ship from Portugal, and for this I needed a permit to cross Spain. As it happened, by the time I obtained a permit for the one, the other would expire, and I would have to go back and get another one. All told, after I had decided to leave, it took almost a year to get everything in order at the proper time.

Fortunately, because I was seventeen, I was granted a Spanish visa. If I had been eighteen, I would not have been able to cross Spain, as that country was one of Hitler's allies. Every eighteen-year-old had to stay there in order later to fight in Hitler's armies.

I failed to get a permit to enter Portugal, where already one hundred thousand refugees were waiting to gain passage to the New World. I missed several ships leaving Lisbon. Finally, having waited from December until July, I decided to leave from Spain instead of from Portugal.

Everything seemed to work out. I could bid farewell to my French friends, leave my French home and board a train for Spain. My aunt Christa and uncle Adolphe Furth from Belgium, who had also escaped to France, were going to meet me in Spain. We were to cross the ocean together.

My uncle Karl financed my trip from Spain to New York. He also sent me fifty dollars to pay for my train fare from France to the port of embarkation in Spain.

In July 1941, I left my French home for America. Hope once gain flickered in my heart.

EUROPE 1938-41
Copyright © Permission from Hammond Inc.

CHAPTER 3
On To America

Once again it was time to say good-bye, this time to my new family who had so willingly taken me in and shared their home with me at the time of my greatest need.

I boarded a train to Spain. I was alone in the compartment and it was hot so I took off my coat. However, I unwisely left my passport and the fifty dollars from uncle Karl in the inside coat pocket. As we crossed the border into Spain, the Spanish police verified my papers and my money. After the inspection I left the compartment for two minutes. When I came back all my money had been stolen! Of course, I could not accuse the Spanish police of stealing it. My ship was scheduled to leave from the coast the next day and I had to catch it. But now I had lost the money to buy a train ticket from Madrid to the coast. A new fear began to grip me that perhaps I would never make it to America.

In Madrid I went from one hotel to another—from one embassy to another—asking for money. At the French Embassy one official offered to buy my Longine wristwatch which my parents had given me as a gift for my confirmation. I refused to part with it. Empty-handed, I moved through the city hoping to find someone who would lend me money. It was a humiliating experience.

After an unsuccessful day, I went to the Madrid police station. I explained to them my need for money. I even asked a policeman whether he wanted to buy some of my precious stamps I had saved. Of course, he refused. Then I asked him whether he would buy a souvenir gold piece.

"To buy gold is forbidden in Spain," he replied firmly. But then he approached me quietly, looked at my gold pieces, and gave me enough money to buy a train ticket to Cadiz where I was to catch the SS Navemar. My uncle and aunt were to meet me in Cadiz where we were going to travel to America together.

In Cadiz another surprise awaited me. I was told the schedule had been changed and the ship was going to leave from Seville. Again I found myself without money for the much needed train ticket. This time a very nice refugee loaned me enough to get to Seville. There, with the last few coins at my disposal, I ordered a horse and buggy, as they did not have taxis. I gave the driver the address of a hotel where my uncle was expected to stay, and off we went. We arrived at the most expensive hotel I had ever seen. At the reception desk I inquired whether my uncle had arrived. I was told they had never heard of him and he was not expected.

I was a seventeen-year-old refugee. I was dirty, exhausted and penniless. I ordered a room. To my surprise they gave me a beautiful room with bath and telephone—unusual in those days and quite expensive. I went to the room and took a wonderful bath.

I realized the serious dilemma I was in. Either my uncle Adolphe would arrive and I would proceed to America, or I would be put in prison because of lack of money and possibly end up in a concentration camp.

Before I went to bed, I knelt in front of my bed and prayed. I had experienced God. He had led me safely from Czechoslovakia to Belgium and He had cared for me during my days as a refugee. He had led me to a French family and He comforted me when I lost my parents. Somehow this all-loving God must have a plan for my life. When I finished my prayer the telephone rang. My aunt and uncle had arrived and were in the lobby! The next day I moved to a cheaper hotel.

I had another interesting experience in Spain during the few days of waiting before our departure. One Sunday I wanted to go to church. I had a difficult time finding a Spanish Protestant church. General Franco, the Spanish dictator, had forbidden Protestant church services. I participated in the worship with about thirty Spaniards. The minister had just returned from a few weeks in prison. Under danger of being sent to prison, they secretly met together in a cellar every Sunday. This service was a moving and unforgettable experience. When people pay such a price for worship, the worship takes on a new depth and meaning. When these people learned I was going to America, they gave me messages and Bibles to take to people in the United States.

At long last we boarded the ship, the SS Navemar, at which point I was flooded with mixed emotions. I truly loved Europe and the people there. I loved my family and my home. America spelled safety and opportunity, but I was saddened at having to leave.

The SS Navemar was a Spanish freighter, a rather small vessel, loaded with nearly 1,100 refugees. When I first saw the ship I wrote in a letter to my grandmother: "I will tell you honestly, for one thousand people, it looks like a very small ship. It will be a terrible trip."

We began the trip with four cattle on board. This would have been enough meat for the voyage. However, we got into a storm and everyone got seasick—the cattle included. The cattle had to be thrown overboard. The diet of the passengers was then limited to rice and potatoes. The trip lasted for forty days, because the ship had to zigzag to avoid German submarines.

I was convinced we would reach America safely. After all, I had arrived in Spain overcoming many obstacles. I felt God's hand on my journey and so I didn't worry. I didn't mind sleeping in lifeboats, not having enough to eat and being sick from time to time. There were other young refugees with whom I played various card games and chess to pass the time. However, the older refugees were worried and concerned about their future. They represented nearly every part of Nazi-occupied Europe and represented all walks of life.

Some refugees could not stand this ordeal and died. For five weeks many hovered between life and death. At last we saw the Statue of Liberty and New York Harbor with all its skyscrapers. We knew our struggles were over and soon a new life would begin for each of us.

Ours was the first large steamer docking in New York loaded with over a thousand refugees who had fled, leaving homes and families behind. Some had been to prison, some had escaped concentration camps. Each of us had suffered.

We were an instant sensation. Many news reporters and photographers greeted us. So this was the America we had heard about. Our pictures appeared in the *New York Daily News* with vivid headlines:

Cattle-Packed Refugees Arrive After Grim Voyage with Death as Stowaway. Ship built to carry 15 passengers, bring 1,120 escapists from Hitler across the Atlantic in Nightmarish trip. The S.S. Navemar is anchored at Quarantine. Packed in like subway passengers, six died en route here. Water was short. One passenger called the food 'garbage.' Another said: 'Only the thought of America kept us alive.' (By a strange trick of fate, the S.S. Navemar was sunk by a submarine on its return voyage to Europe. The refugees who had made this journey to America simply thought, "Navemar—nevermore!")

Excitement surged inside me as I spotted my brother in the crowd. He was actually there. I hadn't seen him for three years. By comparison his experience at times had been more difficult than mine. Being helpless to reach out to me, at times not even knowing where I was or if I were safe, had been a stressful time for him. He had been very much concerned about me, especially after the loss of our parents. He was four years older and was now a student at Columbia University. I was so proud of him. I had always looked up to him.

Cattle-Packed Refugees Arrive After Voyage With Death as Stowaway

John G. Pribram ▼

INFORMATION
Arrivals on the Navemar, fed up with ersatz news published abroad under Hitler, eagerly feast on an American newspaper to learn what's happening in the world.

BOAT-BEDS
These Navemar passengers slept in life boats. Photo was taken by a passenger en route to New York.
Picture of the "Navemar", New York Daily News, September 13, 1941.

Ship Built to Carry 15 Passengers Brings 1,120 Escapists from Hitler Across the Atlantic in Nightmarish Trip

AGONY ON THE ATLANTIC

S.S. Navemar is anchored at Quarantine. Packed in like subway passengers, six died en route here. Water was short. One passenger called the food "garbage." Another said: "Only the thought of America kept us alive."

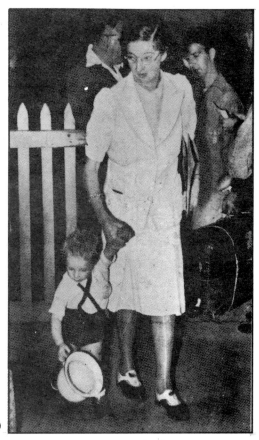

(NEWS photo)

HE TAKES NO CHANCES

When 2-year-old Reni Bravmann disembarked from the S.S. Navemar yesterday with his mother, Mrs. Isabel Bravmann; the young French refugee took no chances with baggagemen in a strange world. He carried his own personal baggage.

He, of course, was anxious to show me the campus and give me a tour of New York City. What an experience. He introduced me to a cafeteria—most convenient for one who does not know the language. I could simply point to the foods I wanted.

We traveled by train to Washington, D.C., where I met my aunt and uncle with whom I was to live for a time. Their apartment was quite small, with no extra room. So, for several weeks, I spent nights on their living room couch. Uncle Karl was an eminent economist working for the U.S. Tariff Commission and gave special lectures at the American University.

I approached America with much concern. I did not know the language. I did not know my aunt and uncle, and I was worried about not being able to make it in college. One of the first things that concerned us was the fact that I had never graduated from high school. Technically I was further advanced in my studies than American college freshmen. With my uncle's help I was offered provisional admittance as a freshman at American University. If I could maintain good grade averages, I would be allowed to stay, if they fell, I would be required to go back to high school.

At the college the students seemed to be more concerned about dates than studies. There they practiced "hazing" which was to make drastic fun of all freshman students.

What a culture shock! I had experienced food rationing and sometimes no food at all. I had lived in a fear of concentration camps and the war, and fear of the future. Now I had all the food I wanted and total freedom and liberty. I realized I was in one of the greatest and most beautiful countries in the world. More and more I felt it was a privilege to live in America and it was a challenge to be worthy of it. I never realized how much it meant to be a free man.

As a foreign student studying at the American University, I was invited to a tea given by Eleanor Roosevelt, the First Lady. She was gracious and welcomed all of us to the United States. It was a moving experience. One day I wondered if I would survive, and the next day I was meeting one of America's foremost leaders.

I was also invited to an "America First" meeting. Honest, sincere people staged the meeting. They believed in isolationism. They wanted America to remain neutral. They were willing to have peace at any price, as long as America would stay out of the war.

I remained silent and kept my thoughts to myself. My experience had taught me a different lesson. Hitler's aims were ruthless. He wanted his Master Race to conquer and rule the world. I realized that only if America would join the British would World War II end with Hitler's defeat.

On December 7th, 1941, I was listening to a philharmonic concert on the radio, presented by Texaco. This enjoyable afternoon was suddenly interrupted by a brief announcement: "The Japanese have attacked Pearl Harbor." The next day the United States declared war against Japan. Hitler's Germany, a Japanese ally, declared war against the United States. World War II had now begun for this my new country!

During the following summer I got my first job. It was in Washington as a Western Union boy delivering telegrams. After my first day of work, I was called to the office. I expected to be fired because I was not an American citizen. To my surprise I was asked to work on Capitol Hill, and I was asked to deliver telegrams to senators and to congressmen. I was able to learn first hand how our American government works. An experience such as this is only possible in a free country.

After two terms at the American University in Washington, D.C., I began to apply for special scholarships offered to refugees. The scholarship I received was from a school in the Midwest, Findlay College in Findlay, Ohio. I was one of the first refugees to come out of Europe to receive a special scholarship there. The faculty, the students, and the community gave me a warm reception.

Very quickly I adjusted to the studies. I majored in chemistry and mathematics. Thanks to good study habits, I receive A's in nearly every course.

I was invited to speak in the college, the community, and many churches about Europe and my personal experiences escaping from Hitler. Often I received generous contributions from various clubs. This was a most welcome supplement to my scholarship funds. My studies were easily financed this way.

I was also invited to become involved in numerous social activities. Before leaving Findlay College, I became president of the student council and president of the student YMCA responsible for a huge fair to benefit the college. In 1944 I was also listed in Who's Who among Students in American Colleges and Universities.

As the war progressed, although I was far removed from it now, I became more and more convinced that this was my war too, and I was intent to do my part. I succeeded in joining the U.S. Army in January 1944.

My convictions were best expressed in a letter to the Findlay College faculty and students reproduced on the front page of the college newspaper:

I am glad to leave and to do my share. I feel my place is with all the other boys who are fighting the enemy and I am glad that my draft board finally decided to take me. But, of course, I hate to leave the college, too. I will never be able to express my appreciation for the swell treatment that I received at the college, because it is impossible to express feelings of gratitude.

During the war I lost everything, but after a few months at Findlay, I came to consider the college as my second home and love it and fight for it. I had a good time at Findlay College; it made me forget the sad time I had in European refugee camps.

Another student responded to my departure from Findlay with a poem:

It was many days ago
In this good old F.C.
That a boy there lived
Whom you may know
By the name of Johnny P.

And this fellow lived with no other thought
Than to study, for studious was he.

He was inexperienced, he did not know
That such no longer is done,
Young people now to college go
For the purpose of having fun.

This college, it changed him, as all can see.
No fact could be more true
But another fact stands out as well
He changed the college too.

And now he is leaving, sincerely we grieve.
We hate to see him go.
But with all our best wishes may he leave,
Since the fate decreed it so.

The Army will change him, of that we are sure
'Twill certainly be so arranged
But we know from the time he's spent with us here,
That the Army by him will be changed.

It was time for yet another good-bye.

Pfc. John G. Pribram

CHAPTER 4
This Is My War, Too

After being inducted into the army, I was trained in a special unit for college students at Fort Benning, Georgia. However, as the war progressed, more infantry was needed and we were transferred to Camp Van Dorn in Mississippi to prepare for tropical warfare. Here I received medical training with the infantry to serve as a medic. The weather was very hot, and we made twenty five-mile marches in the heat.

During this time, since I was willing to go abroad and fight for the United States, my application for citizenship was accelerated and I became an American citizen in Jackson, Mississippi.

The ceremony took place in the Federal Courthouse. It was a simple, straightforward celebration. It filled me with gratitude and hope that this wonderful nation had accepted me and had given me citizenship. I quietly promised to be worthy of this great privilege.

Just as we were preparing for the war in the Pacific, our Division was needed in Europe. We were the first convoy to land in Southern France. It was a memorable experience to enter Marseilles where I previously lived as a refugee—now as part of the Liberation Army.

Marseilles was the very place where I had received my visa to come to America. This was where I had spent hours in front of the U.S. Consulate in an attempt to get this precious piece of paper.

Now I was entering this same city as an American citizen, liberating it from the Nazis. As soon as we landed we were surrounded by children. Chewing gum and chocolates were high in demand. The crowd was exuberant. We were the heroes—the liberators. We were going to help them win the war. As can be imagined, I was much in demand by my buddies since I knew the area and the language.

By Christmas, 1944, our Division—the 63rd Blood and Fire Division—was in Alsace-Lorraine. There, I was asked to be regimental interpreter. Immediately I was moved into a totally different setting. I met German prisoners of war. I saw extensive maps showing the placement of troops and heard talk of the preparation for the offensive. When needed I translated from French and German into English for the officers.

Since our Regiment was a new one, there was as yet no official position for an interpreter. Everything in the U.S. Army was done according to a table of organization. There was no possible way a medic could serve as an interpreter at headquarters. But then someone came up with an idea. The Adjutant of the Regiment told me I could stay on as the interpreter provided I agreed to become the Colonel's orderly as well. When asked what this entailed I was told it meant making the Colonel's bed, setting out his bottle of wine every evening, and tending to his other personal needs.

I refused this new position. I had come to fight a war, not to do things for the Colonel he could do for himself. Of course, I was sent back to my unit. There I became a combat medic attached to the infantry.

I joined my unit just in time to occupy Ribeauville, an Alsatian town. We set up our aid station in a gymnasium. This hall was very dirty. German troops must have lived there before. I had to do something about it. I left in search of a broom. Finally I got one from an Alsatian home. I went back to clean up the hall. As I worked, I had a crazy thought: Whatever would happen to me from now on, I would carry the broom with me.

The next day we moved into the mountains and climbed up to the ridge which divided us from the enemy. I was still carrying my broom.

For the night I found a cave. It was much better than digging a foxhole myself. As I surveyed the terrain, I spotted a dead German, partly covered with snow, not fifteen feet from my cave. This was the first dead German I had ever seen. Hardened by the war experiences, I didn't think much about him or his family. They would not know his fate for a long time. I withdrew to my cave for the night.

Fear filled my heart and the hearts of our men. As it grew darker, we waited to see if the Germans would attack us. We were alert to the smallest noise, to footsteps or shadows. When rifle fire was exchanged, I was forced to venture out, hiding behind trees and bushes, to see if our men were in position and unharmed.

Fortunately, only one man was wounded in the arm. I bandaged him, gave him morphine, and sent him back down the hill to the aid station.

Later, I was to think of the strange contrasts of war: in the midst of gunfire, death, pain and fear, there I was with my silly broom.

The next day we were ordered to leave the mountain range, return to the Alsatian town, and receive a more dangerous assignment.

We were called in early the next morning. Our unit had failed to take a hill essential in the battle for the city of Colmar. A new strategy was being developed. Since the straight approach to take the hill from the Germans had failed, we were asked to cross a minefield and attack the hill from the other side.

The new approach was considered extremely dangerous. The combat medics were discouraged from going. It takes a long time to train a medic, and headquarters did not want unnecessary losses. However, each of the medics, myself included, chose to stay with our men and support them in this daring adventure.

We started in the early morning hours. The hills were covered with snow. For weeks we had trained in the heat to prepare us for tropical warfare, and now we found ourselves in the bitter cold. We were issued white uniforms to avoid being detected by the enemy. Our unit moved slowly across the field. The men with the mine detectors first, then one soldier following in the footsteps of the other-the medics last.

Suddenly the enemy saw us. The sound of machine gun fire ripped through the early morning quiet, we were forced to disperse. Many soldiers set off mines and were wounded. Now my job as a medic began. I was helping someone when I heard a scream. I rushed through the fog in the direction of the dying man. On the way I stepped on a "schu-mine" and was blown into the air.

I realized I was seriously wounded. I dared not put a tourniquet around my leg for fear I would pass out and the tourniquet would do more harm than good. For eight hours we lay in the snow, suffering from shock and exposure, waiting to be rescued.

I couldn't understand it. I knew God had saved me many times before and had led me in a miraculous way from Czechoslovakia to the United States. But I hadn't done anything with my life yet. Surely it couldn't all end on a snowy, bloodstained hillside in France.

As we lay there waiting, each soldier was filled with his own private fears. Our own aid station had orders not to come to our rescue because the area was too dangerous. The possibility of being taken prisoner was very real. I wondered, as a native of Czechoslovakia, how would the Germans treat me? Would I yet end up in a concentration camp? Or perhaps we would all lie there, suffering in pain and cold, until we died…

But I prayed. God had led me in such an amazing way already—He would lead me still. Slowly I felt faith overtaking the anxieties.

It was an unbelievable moment of joy when our men made their way precariously back across that minefield to rescue us. They had taken the hill from the Germans, and now they were coming back for us. I shall never cease to be grateful. The men I had known for only a few months risked their very lives to carry the other wounded men and me to safety.

From the battlefield I was carried to an aid station. By this time I was suffering from exposure and was in extreme pain. I had lost a great deal of blood and required several blood transfusions. It seemed the chills would never end. Drugs were administered to ease the blinding pain. In the midst of it all, a sergeant came by and tossed a little box on my stomach. I opened it. There lay the PURPLE HEART.

From the aid station I was transported to a hospital near Marseilles. There I received the sobering news—my leg could not be saved. They would have to amputate. After the surgery I experienced less pain and was beginning to feel somewhat better.

However, when I was allowed to leave my bed and I walked on crutches for the first time, I was devastated. The shock of my loss hit me full force. I broke down and cried uncontrollably. I was a cripple, I would never be the same again.

The outgrowth of this shock was a new bitterness, especially against the Germans. I began to blame them for everything. My hatred spawned sarcasm, and the weapon I used to vent my hostilities was my tongue.

In the hospital were many German prisoners of war. Some were patients, and some were orderlies. I went out of my way to speak to them in German and tell them of our most recent Allied victories. It was a cheap way to hurt others, and I look back upon it today with a great deal of shame.

Later, a friend of mine shared with me that during this time of my bitterness and sarcasm, and my searching for a way of life and answers to problems, I had all the makings of a communist.

For the action in the minefield, all involved received the third highest decoration of the U.S. Army, the SILVER STAR.

My citation reads:

For gallantry in action on January 24, 1945, in the vicinity of Bennwihr, France, with utter disregard for his personal safety Pfc. John G. Pribram entered a known schu-mine field, rendering aid to wounded men. Exhibiting great courage and bravery and acting under heavy rifle, machine pistol, machine gun, mortar and artillery fire, he continued to render aid to the wounded, until he sustained the loss of a foot, due to a schu-mine explosion.

As I waited in Marseilles for the hospital ship to take me back to the states, I was visited by Mme Ameye, the mother of the French family who had taken me in as a young refugee. What a wonderful reunion that was! She and the family had survived the war and she had gone to great lengths to be with me because transportation was scarce in those war years. She cheered me by telling me they had kept my bicycle as a special antique-souvenir! To the present day I have remained in touch with the sons of that very special family.

At last, I made my return journey across the Atlantic—in a hospital ship rather than a crowded freighter—I was sent to the McGuire General Hospital in Richmond, Virginia. There my long process of rehabilitation and recovery would begin.

CHAPTER 5
After Combat

To fight the war against the Nazis was one thing, but once the war was over, emptiness filled the hearts of many veterans like myself. I found it was much easier to be against something—to criticize, agitate and fight, than to have creative answers and know what to live for.

This was a basic underlying problem in the hospital. We had fought the war. Some of us had been severely wounded, losing the use of an arm or leg, or both legs, or were blind. We faced the future with much uncertainty and fear. Would we ever be accepted as normal human beings? Was the war—which had just ended with the defeat of Hitler—to be the beginning of a time of peace? Or was there an increased danger of world communism?

The days spent in the hospital gave me much time to think, much time for self-analysis.

I was not sorry I had served my country in the armed forces. It had given me great pride to return to Europe as an American soldier. Joining the army meant I was willing to pay any price to get rid of an evil dictatorship and win the war for democracy. I would have done it all over again had it been necessary. Nevertheless, I was not prepared for the feeling of self-pity and uselessness that struck me as I struggled through recuperation.

All the veterans at the hospital were generally experiencing these feelings. The deep basic desires of mankind to become like others, to be liked by others and to be approved of by others can be so strong and paralyzing that if a person yields to those desires, he may well miss his real calling.

Among the many visitors to the hospital there was a group of young people. They came to sing for the veterans. I was impressed by them. They were different from other visitors. They didn't talk about trivial matters, they didn't come to pity us for what happened in combat. In fact, it didn't seem they wanted anything for themselves. They were spreading friendship, hope, and a sense of purpose.

I talked with them and they came back for more visits. They taught me a very simple truth that helped me see my life in the right perspective:

God has a plan for the world, for every nation and for every person. When man listens, God speaks to him through his conscience. When man obeys his innermost thoughts, provided they measure up to absolute moral values of honesty, purity, love and unselfishness as expressed in the Sermon on the Mount,

God acts and man changes. As man changes, nations change and a New World is built.

Among those young people I met, two of them were sisters. They talked much about their pastor, Dr. Lev Evans. At one point they challenged my thinking to the degree that I gave Dr. Evans a call.

I was highly impressed when this busy minister dropped what he was doing and came to visit that very day. In this gentle pastor I saw a genuine mark of a Christian—a person willing to live what he talked. This challenged me more than anything else.

The seeds of Christianity had been planted deep within my heart as a young person. And now at a point where I was questioning everything in life, this pastor and others like him came into my life.

The pastor suggested that the best way to keep listening and obeying was to write down my thoughts in a quiet meditation time, preferably in the early morning before starting the day.

The new concepts I was learning sounded good, but I was severely tested the day I was scheduled to learn to walk on my artificial leg. For someone who has lost a leg, the first day of walking is of vital importance. It answers the basic question: Will I once again be like everyone else?

When I attempted to walk for the first time with my artificial leg, it did not work. I was absolutely crushed. I felt miserable and lonely. In utter despair, I decided to follow my friend's counsel and write down all my thoughts.

I started out blaming the doctors and the nurses for doing such a poor job. Then I blamed the American Government. Finally I just blamed everyone I could think of for my sad condition.

However, as I continued writing, my thinking turned around. I thought of God and how much He had helped me throughout my life and how grateful I was for many things I had experienced. At one point, I wrote a startling thought: "Have faith, everything is going to be different."

The next day I went to see the doctor. I tried out the artificial leg, and I could walk! Since that day, I have never experienced any difficulty in walking.

This was my first real attempt at having a time of quiet meditation. I have tried it many times since that afternoon in the hospital. I discovered that I need not be in a ditch with bombs falling all around, or penniless in Spain, or in a foxhole in combat to receive help from God. I could turn to Him everyday and search for ways to do His will.

A new journey—or perhaps a more consistent continuation of the old journey—had begun.

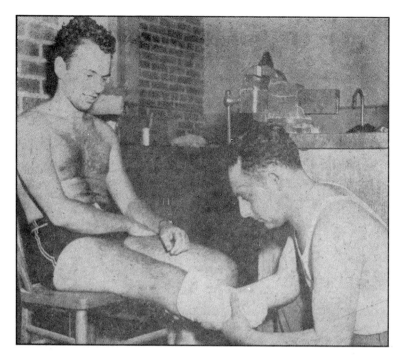

Pfc. John G. Pribram of Washington, D.C., patient in Ward 2, receives a cast fitting for an artificial leg from Pvt. Norman Palmer of Monessen, Pa. Pfc. Pribram, who wears the Silver Star for "gallantry in action," lost his leg last January during the battle for Colmar, France. Johnny, whose Czechoslovakian parents were slain by the Nazis, was a senior in college when he entered the Army to serve as an overseas combat medic.

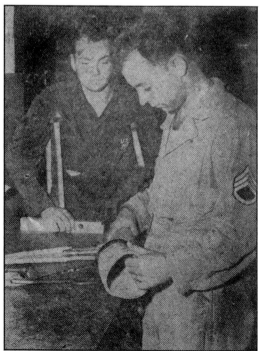

The artificial leg socket is being fitted to Johnny's stump measure by S/Sgt. Alfred Sulinia, of Philadelphia, Pa.

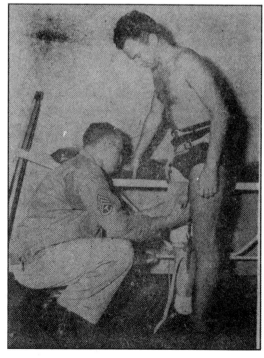

Tec 3 Jack Twiford of Hampton, Va., fits the completed leg as Johnny tries it on "for size."

McGuire General Hospital, McGuire Banner, August 10, 1945

My friends who had helped me in the hospital invited me to an International Conference for the Moral Re-Armament of Nations on Mackinac Island in Michigan. There I met people from all walks of life and from different nations. They did not simply talk about democracy; they tried to follow it in their personal lives at home, on the job and for their country.

This is what I had been looking for, it was a practical answer to bitterness, hatred, division, and wars. I decided to put into practice all I had been learning at the conference.

To become part of the cure in the world meant putting right what was wrong in my own life and then fighting for what's right at home, among friends, in this nation, and in the world.

During my stay in the hospital, I had become embittered against civilians for showing little or no appreciation for veterans. This attitude was extremely divisive and a change was needed.

I blamed our leaders for wars, and yet, I had a longstanding feud with a cousin of mine that divided my own family. I swallowed my pride and apologized to my cousin for my jealousies and wrongdoings. We became friends again.

To put things right I knew I had to talk to the head of the Science Department at Findlay College. He had been one of the most feared professors on campus, and I had been one of his best students. But once I had lied to him and I now realized I must make it right. An invitation to return and speak to the students gave me the opportunity. As I approached the door to his office I was nervous. I sent up a quick prayer, then I moved in and faced the professor. I apologized for my dishonesty. He was overwhelmed. Something like this had never happened to him. My visit affected even his attitude towards other students.

I had blamed our government for being dishonest; yet, upon discharge from the Army Hospital I took a beautiful morning coat, crutches, and towels with me. I rationalized as a disabled veteran, I had the right to keep them. However, if every veteran took things that belonged to the government, wasn't that part of the dishonesty and corruption? As part of my ongoing acts of restitution I mailed the various items back to the hospital with a brief note.

Now I was able to pen some of my basic new convictions. The following was published in the *Richmond Times Dispatch* on November 12, 1945, as "Observations of an Amputee."

It is almost a year since I lost my leg while fighting as a combat medic in the European Theater of Operation.

When I first started to go to town on crutches, I was quite often affected by the look of pity the civilians had or some questions they were asking me. Thus, I became depressed and started to pity myself, thinking that nobody really cared for us combat veterans.

Soon I became happier, because I learned how to walk and I could go to town without being noticed too much. What I wanted most was to be considered as normal and as a future civilian.

Nevertheless I was looking with anxiety towards my first 45-day furlough, wondering how I might get along with my artificial leg among all those civilians.

Well, I got along OK, my leg was perfect, thanks to the training the hospital had provided for us amputees.

But I noticed quite a few things. I was shocked by the normal way people were living. Nobody seemed to care much about the war we just finished and nobody seemed to know much about combat and the returning veterans. Yes, the contrast between the environment of rough combat men, who almost died for their country and the civilians, was immense.

How much was I doing to change it? I discovered that my attitude towards civilians was wrong too. I was somewhat looking down on them and even despising them for not having gone through the mill I did.

Soon I discovered that my honest sharing of my combat experiences as well as my honest criticism could contribute towards unity and decrease the gap between civilians and G.I.'s. Thus I learned it was better to explain to a civilian who was pitying me, that this attitude wasn't helping either one of us, that both of us were normal, and that we needed to fight together for peace..

Finally, I discovered that life back in the states is as rough and rugged as combat, with the only difference that in combat the Jerry and the Jap were our enemies, while now any evil thought in myself as well as in others is our enemy.

In combat, while hugging the ground, I was praying to God to help me, He did. While out of the hospital in "cold, selfish" world, I discovered the need of complete trust and confidence in God.

The battle—line between right and wrong is clear-cut in my heart, and I see that in spite of the fact that I lost my leg, I still owe plenty to my country. The fight for peace has just begun.

Peace is not an idea; it's people becoming different. By changing my outlook about almost everything, by thinking, 'Is this constructive or destructive?' I saw clearly how I could fight for others.

The trouble with the world is that we are much too selfish. Thus I decided to change my outlook and attempted to get over my own selfishness and learned to live on a basis of absolute honesty and pure love for all people. Doing that, it is certainly easier to get along with all people—G.I. as well as civilians.

The battle for peace, the war of ideas is on. A tough fight awaits every one of us, more dangerous than the war of arms, but more important.

During my visit to Findlay College, it was a joy to see many old friends and make new ones. The *Findlay College Y-Zette* expressed my views, "Outlook of a G.I. Joe", on October 26, 1945.

What an immense privilege to come back to good old Findlay College and spend a couple of weeks with you. The college pulled through the crises successfully and is recovering rapidly. But let us not get self-satisfied. Combat and overseas service showed me clearly that it is a challenge for us to be Christians.

Today, I see clearly the necessity for teamwork and sincere cooperation with everyone whom I come in contact, especially those I never used to like. I have to think in terms of how much can I give to others, instead of what I can get out of it. Only by getting along with people, by understanding them and loving them, can I help in building unity here at Findlay College as well as anywhere in the world.

Before I joined the Army I thought it was good enough to be a jolly good fellow. Well the world has changed. It is not enough for me to call on God in foxholes and forget Him while I think I am safe. Finally I realized that we are living in an emergency and only unlimited faith can answer all our problems.

I can't sit back and rest anymore and let someone else do the thinking for me. No, I have to strive to be an active Christian. The way I live, think and act, might be the way 130 million Americans might think and act, too.

If I decided to think about my comforts and selfish aims first, others might do the same and I am the root of the division here and in my country; but if I care for others more than myself, if I practice Christ's teaching, others might do the same. United as a team we will fight together, not only for a sound home and a sound nation, but a New World controlled by God.

After my discharge from the Army, I took advantage of the G.I. Bill of Rights and continued my education at Harvard. I felt I could make a greater contribution in human relations than in science, so I switched my major to government and history. I was determined to make good use of my valuable experience I had had.

As war veterans there was only one thing we wanted to do: quickly finish our studies and graduate. To keep up my French, I joined the French Club and later became its president. However, my social life was kept to a minimum. In fact, I remember one Fourth of July when several in our rooms studying, heard firecrackers going off, we thought it was an air raid and were ready to dive for cover. To our relief we realized it was a holiday. We quickly went down the Charles River and enjoyed a most fabulous display!

In June 1947, I received my degree from Harvard. Our graduation speaker was Secretary of State George C. Marshall. At this memorable occasion he proclaimed the now-famous Marshall Plan, a plan that helped to bring about the Reconstruction of Western Europe and saved Western Europe from being taken over by Communism.

At Harvard, one of our guest speakers was Jan Masaryk, son of the founder of Czechoslovakia and Foreign Minister from 1945-48. He hoped his country could become the bridge between East and West. He wanted his country to participate in the Marshall Plan, but Moscow forced Czechoslovakia to stick with the Communist policies.

I visited Masaryk in his office at the United Nations. He could have stayed in the West, but he returned to Prague in an attempt to make the vision he had for his country a reality. Just prior to the final Communist takeover, Masaryk's body was found on the pavement beneath his bedroom window. It has never been determined whether it was suicide or an assassination. But his death was the beginning of the complete takeover of Czechoslovakia by the Communist.

A NOTE ON MORAL RE-ARMAMENT

Moral Re-Armament was launched in 1938 when Europe was rearming. Frank Buchman, MRA's American initiator, called for a programme of 'moral and spiritual rearmament' to address the root causes of conflict, and work toward a 'hate-free, fear-free, greed-free world'. Since then people of all backgrounds and traditions have been active in this program on every continent.

MRA is open to all. Its starting point is the readiness of each person to make real in their own life the changes they wish to see in society. A commitment to search for God's will in daily life forms the basis for creative initiative and common action. Absolute moral standards of honesty, purity, unselfishness and love help to focus the challenge of personal and global change.

"For A Change" April/May, 1999

PART II:
Post War Reconstruction

CHAPTER 6
The Work Begins

During the summer of 1948, I was involved with a musical revue called *"The Good Road."* The revue consisted of humorous sketches of contemporary life in home and industry, plus a moving pageant of history featuring such figures as Moses, Joan of Arc, Abraham Lincoln and others. The writers attempted to bring out the best of history for each country. The musical proclaimed dramatically the basic ideas of freedom and the necessary conditions of a sound society.

Young people from many nations expressed in song and dance their convictions for the future. "Sorry Is A Magic Little Word" pointed a way for brothers and sisters to get along with one another. Not left, not right, but straight ahead on *"The Good Road."* A glimpse of the future was given where all races from all nations work together in mutual understanding to create a world of peace and happiness.

Members of the troupe were delighted when we were invited to an International Conference at Caux in Switzerland. This was to be a historic occasion, as well as a major turning point in my life.

There at Caux, for the first time since the war, Germans were also participating. Most of them had not been out of their country since 1933. The German delegation consisted of 500 members including twelve cabinet ministers from the various German Land government. More than 5,000 people from fifty different countries participated at the Caux assembly.

In early October following our participation in the conference, a cable came from Dr. Karl Arnold, the Minister-President of North Rhine Wesphalia and his cabinet inviting a task force of Moral Re-Armament to visit the Ruhr bringing with them *"The Good Road."* Dr. Arnold's aim was to "spread the spirit of Caux in our land, and thereby give our nation new hope and new strength." Similar invitations came from the Minister-Presidents of Bavaria, Wurttemberg-Baden and Baden-Baden.

To go back to Europe was the last thing I ever wanted to do. I had escaped from there and had fought there in combat. I did not want to go back again. However, I did want to do something worthwhile with my life. I could have carried on with my studies in Political Science and received a master's degree from Harvard University.

To accept this invitation to Germany became a real test of the sincerity of my convictions. I had talked about the peace of the world, about helping other people, and even other countries. But deep in my heart there was still much bitterness against the country responsible for the death of my parents and the occupation of my native land. I still blamed the Germans for disrupting the peaceful time I had had in Czechoslovakia and for starting a war in which the whole world had been involved.

Factually those accusations seemed right, but after much thought, study and research, I had to accept that some of the seeds of World War II were sown after World War I. Germany was not the only responsible power for World War I, as the 1919 Treaty of Versailles seemed to indicate. The severe punishment of Germany as the only guilty power created within that country frustration, bitterness, and a deep desire to accept a leader who promised to take their country a great nation again. It is true the German people were fooled by their new leader, Adolf Hitler, but so was the rest of the world, a fact that was revealed in the book "Reaching For the Stars" by American author Nora Wahlin.

Following World War I, the United States could have played a leading part in securing the peace that had been gained. However, we refused to join the League of Nations, a newly created International Organization. We decided to follow the traditional policy of "Isolationism." In fact, we passed trade laws, especially the Hawley-Smoot Tariff Act of 1930, which provided for a high protective tariff that made it virtually impossible for Europe to sell goods to America. Europe was unable to pay her debts to us and recover economically.

As I reviewed this information I remembered how I had treated with sarcasm and bitterness, the Germans I met during World War II. I also had to accept the fact that some of the persecution of the Germans in Czechoslovakia, immediately after the war, was similar to the horrors committed by the Nazis during the war. Two million Sudenten—Germans were expelled from Czechoslovakia by the Communist—inspired Czech Government!

This convinced me that hatred and bitterness are not the monopoly of one group of people—these human forces are at work in every one of us. It is not a question of class, religion or race; the basic issue is character.

In spite of all my logical reasoning, it took me a week of contemplation to set aside my bitterness and then wholeheartedly accept the invitation to travel to Europe and participate in the social and moral reconstruction of post-war Europe.

Even though we had a formal invitation to come to Germany, permission still had to be secured from the military authorities. That permission was granted by both the American and the British military for a civilian task force of many nations to enter Germany. It was the first International force to go in, and I was to be part of it.

The Germany that we were traveling to had been totally ravaged by the war. In the three years since the war, there had been little or no rebuilding. Many cities still lay in rubble. There had been three years of strong military control. No one trusted the Germans and, until Caux, no Germans had been permitted to participate at international conferences.

The country was divided into four zones occupied by American, British, French, and Soviet forces. Cities and towns were ruled by Allied Military troops and food was very scarce.

Berlin, which lay 110 miles inside the Russian zone, was likewise divided into four sectors with each of the Big Four controlling one sector. The Western Allies were guaranteed access to Berlin by surface and air routes across the Russian zone. Initially this division was said to be temporary.

The Eastern provinces of Germany were detached from Germany with part occupied by Russia, but most placed under Polish control. This resulted in a mass exodus of Germans who chose not to live under communism. These refugees swarmed into West Germany where the economic conditions were already at a standstill.

Hundreds of thousands of Germans were in prisoner-of-war camps and were only released once they were cleared of their Nazi past. Trials were held across the country as war criminals were brought to justice.

The Western powers and the U.S.S.R. claimed to favor Re-unification of Germany, but disagreed as to the methods for such Re-unification. In 1948 the Western powers combined their zones and the military government was slowly replaced by German officials appointed by military to be in charge of villages, town and cities. Local elections were permitted, and very slowly local and state governments emerged in Western Germany.

In September 1948, there was a constitutional assembly in Bonn, West Germany, to create a Federal Republic of Germany; Dr. Konrad Adenauer became the first Chancellor of postwar Germany.

Meanwhile, in the Eastern Sector Communism was gaining a stronger and stronger foothold.

It was during this time of growth, change and rebirth that the Moral Re-Armament group entered Germany. Our task was to show our German friends that there was hope and that together we could fight for a way of life that would be more exciting and more fruitful than National Socialism, Communism, or just plain "paper" democracy. It was our desire to live a life so contagious that people would feel that democracy was practical and "that it would be lived."

Our task force was made up of 250 people from many different countries. As the cast presented the revue in Munich and in Stuttgart, I was among a group of six who traveled ahead to Frankfurt to prepare for the next performance in Frankfurt.

General Lucius Clay, Commander-in-chief of the American Occupation Forces, chose to suport their German Leaders invitation to bring *"The Good Road"* to Germany. As a result the U.S. Army was fully behind our efforts. We traveled under order like G.I.'s but with the privileges of civilians. Staff cars were at our disposal.

Kenaston Twitchell who earlier had made all the initial arrangements with General Clay best describes the conditions that faced us in Frankfort.

Frankfurt used to be a beautiful town, but much of it has been completely destroyed during the war. Parts of the city look like ghost towns. A very tragic sight. The Römerplatz, the heart of Frankfurt, consists of ruins and more ruins, trees growing out of houses. The famous cathedral is partly destroyed. Ruble is everywhere, usually piled up to the second floor, behind gaping shells of walls. Yet, even there, you occasionally see signs of habitation as people tried to find shelter. The central railroad station is a mass of twisted steel, yet somehow trains are running.

Across from the station we found a hotel, most of it still intact. Nearby is a U.S. Army car parking lot, closely guarded and ringed with barbed wire. We soon learned that anything left unguarded for a few minutes was likely to disappear. People are starving and have little hesitancy in stealing from the conqueror that seems to have everything.

Most of the theaters had been destroyed. As a result, locating a facility in which to represent the revue was our foremost challenge. The only possible place we found was the Palmengarten, which was being used as an Army Club. It had a very small stage, and technically, it was impossible to present the production there. But the army provided engineers, and a new stage was built. The Army cancelled a G.I. event to give us the place for Sunday. Then the Mayor of Frankfurt cancelled a concert for another day.

However, a German magician had rented the stage for an evening, and when he was asked by the Minister of Education to cancel, he refused.

We decided to pay a visit to the magician. For an hour and a half he talked to us, complaining about the dreadful situation in Germany. He compared it with 1933. Even under Hitler, he said things were better. He was bitter at the present German leadership, but grateful for the Americans. He was filled with mixed feelings.

Finally, when he was prepared to listen, we explained to him our task, and the fact that we wanted to help rebuild Germany. He was amazed and promptly gave up the stage for us.

There were also difficulties getting invitations printed, but we located a printer who had printing presses that had not bee damaged, even though the building in which they were housed was badly demolished on the outside. The leader of the Christian Democratic party allowed us to use his office so that we could send out the invitations and his youth group was asked to work with us.

At times, I acted as an interpreter. I also helped with invitations and tickets and worked with the German students to organize ushering at the theater. Many of the young people that I met during that time agreed it was time for all German youth to begin looking beyond their own problems and begin to reach out and help others.

One young man I met wanted to join in and help, but his father-in-law (who was also his employer) objected. I explained to him that unity at home was part of our principles and that unity was more important than his help in the office. The young man then repeated this conversation to his father-in-law. The older man was very impressed and agreed then for the son-in-law to work with us.

Distribution of the tickets was handled by the Finance Director of Bizonia (British/American zones). He put his office at our disposal and his secretaries took care of the distribution.

When the 250 member troupe arrived in Frankfurt, they were billeted under army orders in army barracks in hotels in Frankfurt and in Bad-Homburg, a pre-war vacation spot. The Commanding General of this area had a staff meeting to determine how the details of accommodations, food, transport and theater arrangements would be arranged. Leading Germans and top U.S. officials cooperated together, then all of them came to see "The Good Road."

We had army food for our meals. It was adequate and good. One day a German friend invited me to a German restaurant. We needed tickets for fats, meat and bread, which were still being rationed in Germany. My meal consisted of soup, tomatoes filled with meat, and no dessert. The cost was eleven (Deutsche Mark), approximately $3.25, which in 1948 was very expensive. A vast difference from the abundance of food for the American soldiers.

In a letter to my family I made clear how these conditions disturbed me:

Germany today seems to me to show two different worlds. The Americans live in a dream world, with everything they want, much more than they need—from hot dogs to hamburgers and milkshakes, special arrangements for Christmas shopping, etc. The other world is the dark world of a defeated people—hatred and bitterness, little food, immense difficulties and over-crowded living quarters.

The American world ignores the German world, takes advantage of it and helps in decreasing the morale of the people German. Marks mean very little. Cigarettes and chocolate are everything.

"The Good Road" was an unbelievable success. The spirit of the revue was the talk of the town. For the first time the Germans felt the extended hand of their conquerors and they were finding hope that there could be a better future. The press coverage was very good with nearly sixty newspapermen attending the shows. Radio Frankfurt recorded the songs of "The Good Road", and from the money paid to us we were able to pay the orchestra.

Because of limited space many people were turned away from the theatre. As I turned them away I said, "As an American, I am sorry. We have destroyed the Opera; we have destroyed your big theaters. That's why we have to present "The Good Road" here in the Palmengarten. That's why there is not enough space for all of you to come in." These Germans may have never heard an American apologize to them before.

One evening after the show I met a young man who had been brought up under Hitler and had been a Nazi for a short period. Under the "Denazification Law" he was required to report this. But his parents urged him not to, for fear something bad would happen to him if he confessed. My new friend was very concerned as to what to do. On one hand his parents were urging him not to admit the faults of the past, on the other hand, his own conscience and the new law of the land dictated him to confess his actions. Watching "The Good Road" he saw the inner freedom and the true inner peace he had been look-ing for. He left there determined to make the right decision.

I made many friends in Frankfurt, especially among the young people. Through painful honesty among family members some had found answers to their broken homes. The Frankfurt chief of police expressed his desire to let all the juvenile delinquents of the city see the show. The policemen, who were supposed to help prevent overcrowding, were letting people into the theatre through special doors.

In a letter to my grandmother, I wrote:

The main problem here, and continuously so, is to learn to put myself into the shoes of a German. His cities are destroyed. Americans are taking out their women. Americans eat where Germans are not allowed to go. Americans have everything.

I try to think how I would feel in America if another country occupied our land. If American girls were being raped by foreign soldiers, if there would be signs everywhere banning Americans from entering, and if adequate food were available only for the occupying forces. That's the way some of the Germans feel about America and Russia. To change this outlook is a difficult task.

The Germans may have deserved this fate, but now it is important to dispel hatred and become a family of nations.

It was hard to leave Frankfurt. The impact of "The Good Road" there had been overwhelming. Now we were moving into the British Zone which was more like England, we would not have one hundred percent backing from the U.S. Army.

As we traveled northward, we stopped at the famous Kronberg Castle where German nobility used to live. I stayed in the room of her Majesty, the Empress Frederick, former princess of Great Britain. Since the U.S. Army had temporarily taken over the castle, I paid only fifty cents for the room.

In the afternoon we visited a beautiful farm, which belonged to a German colonel. There fifty Sudeten Germans had found a new home. I recalled that over two million Sudeten Germans had been expelled from Czechoslovakia at the end of World War II. Some barely made it across the border and had lost everything.

I met a Sudeten German whose parents had died escaping the Czechs. He had lost his home and his native country. I said to him, "I am sorry for what my countrymen did to you. Please forgive us." Then I explained my similar experiences with the Nazis. It was amazing that this young man found freedom from bitterness and hatred and found new hope for his country and for all of Europe.

On our way to the Ruhr we stopped in Cologne. There the cathedral, virtually untouched by bombs, stood in the midst of ruins. There were blocks and blocks of ruins; yet life went on. An unforgettable sight!

The ruins in the Ruhr were as devastating as in the other cities where we had traveled. But it was not just the buildings that had suffered. When four sixteen-year-old boys took advantage of a fifteen-year-old girl, a policeman said there was nothing he could do about it. "They are just having fun," he replied. Such conditions were heartrending.

In the Ruhr the Finance Minister took care of the entire operation; he sent out the invitations. The Minister of Food felt responsible for the feeding of the 250 guests, and the chief of the Press Section took care of the publicity.

The chairman of the trade unions, responsible for three to four million workers, endorsed the showing of *"The Good Road"*. He had said that the bitterness and hatred needed to be addressed before it was too late.

The showings were scheduled for Düsseldorf, Essen and Dortmund. Here the response was similar to that in Frankfurt. Everyone seemed pleased by the visit of this first International Force.

Minister-President Arnold, who was in constant communication with us, reported that *"The Good Road"* was talked about in homes, offices, and factories. Many lives were touched and changed. One young man named Walter had joined the German Army at the age of fifteen. For a year and a half he suffered as a prisoner of the Russians—at times on a starvation diet. Three times he tried to escape, but he was caught each time and beaten by the communists. Finally he did escape to Berlin and went on foot to the west, swimming across the Elbe River, and successfully located his parents. However, it was not until he saw *"The Good Road"* that he discovered a hope in life. He had never got along with his sister, but he took her to see the show and they were united. When he became honest with his parents, it was a new beginning. His mother remarked that it was the happiest day of her life. Walter had thought there was nothing but expectations of war in the future, but this has been replaced by a faith in a better world.

Later, as invitations came from Holland and England, the cast made preparations to leave Germany. Meanwhile several cast members myself included, had been invited by the Minister-President of North Rhine Westphalia and his cabinet to stay on in Germany. We were asked to help the Germans create an industrial drama, *"The Forgotten Factor"*, and to continue to spread the new spirit of practical democracy.

I was faced with a new decision. I had been traveling with *"The Good Road"* for many months; we were like a family. It would be difficult to see them go home, but I felt certain my place was to be in Germany to help the German people.

CHAPTER 7
In Germany 1948-49

It was difficult to see the "gang" move on to Holland and England while I stayed behind with a smaller group.

Of the ones who stayed behind there was Kennie, the grandson of a U.S. senator who had interrupted his education at Princeton to be a part of the work;

Bill, a former officer of the U.S. Army of Occupation; Jens, a student from Oslo University, who had fought in the resistance during the war; Betty, the daughter of a Dutch banker; and Max, a French mechanic who lost family members in Nazi concentration camps. We were joined by a German kindergarten teacher, a former Hitler youth leader, a son of a German general and many others. All of them had experienced God at work in their lives and wanted to make democracy a practical way of life for Germany. We were from a wide variety of backgrounds, and were ready to work with this new task force.

One young student, who joined our cast, was Frowin. Frowin was typical of many of the youth of Germany. He had been brought up in a Christian home, and was in grade school when Hitler took over Germany. As the Nazi movement expanded, the best young people were invited to summer camps in the mountains. Frowin qualified to go. At the camp he enjoyed a variety of sports and never noticed the Nazi propaganda being taught there.

When the war started, every youngster wanted to fight for his country, so Frowin joined the armed forces. Naturally, he expected his country to win. At no time did Frowin suspect the Jews were being persecuted and put into concentration camps. Those facts were disclosed after Germany was defeated. Everything in his world had collapsed. The nation was guilty and Frowin was part of the nation.

Shattered and in despair, Frowin turned to God—the God he had prayed to as a child. He found a new joy and a new freedom. Later, he became a vital part of the Moral Re-Armament team.

Because Düsseldorf was so heavily destroyed, several of us lived on a ship brought in from Holland and anchored in the Rhine. The food there was simple, but not bad. Lack of food and accommodations continued to be an ever-present problem. I wrote home for my family and friends to "send all possible food parcels. The winter promises to be cold and there is not much food *in the British Zone of Occupation."*

We produced a play in German called "*The Forgotten Factor*". It was written for presentation in industrial areas. The plot of the play disclosed how a strike situation was aggravated by a communist-led faction in the union. It portrayed the courageous actions of individuals on both sides, leading to the resolution of the industrial conflict and foiling the extremists' plans to take control of the industry. The play described in a simple way the roots of bitterness and dishonesty that lead to class warfare and strikes.

In the play an alternative was suggested by the son of the factory owner who had discovered "*The Forgotten Factor*" in human relations namely honesty and resolution of the wrongs of the past. It led to a solution based on the principle, "It's not *who* is right, but *what* is right," and that this approach would solve complicated and difficult situations. God is the forgotten factor!

To prepare for "*The Forgotten Factor*" we needed help from the community. High school students, mostly seniors who had seen *"The Good Road"* were ready to meet with us and help in the preparation of the show. They sent out invitations, provided hospitality, and gave out programs at the performances.

Two of these students told us that their entire Latin class had decided to stop cheating, pay streetcar fares, and change in various other ways. A new spirit was spreading through their homes and the school. Briefly, they had changed from discouraged, unhappy youth to youth with a passion and a plan for the future.

The business community helped also. The Chamber of Commerce donated funds, the Coal Board provided for our meals, the City Hall employed eight people to address envelopes and distribute tickets. In addition, cars were provided for our transportation.

The premiere took place in Essen, an industrial city that was eighty percent destroyed in the war. The Minister-President, Dr. Karl Arnold and the Mayor of Essen, Gustav Heineman, introduced the show to an overcrowded audience. It was a tremendous success.

Simple things such as a warm room, a bath, or even enough hot water for shaving were luxuries, but the warmhearted reception from German families was overwhelming.

From Essen we moved to the beautiful mining town of Datteln. The mine manager and the chairman of the works council were guided by the same principals described in "*The Forgotten Factor*". They along with the city officials were working as a team. Together they had invited us to come. The mines paid for our food and we lived in homes scattered throughout Datteln.

As before, the show had a tremendous impact. It became the talk of the town. A leading communist changed from his class warfare outlook. A newspaperman, a former Nazi leader said, "If only we would have known about how to practice democracy some fifteen years ago, all that mess could have been avoided. Now we must work fast and build a sound foundation. I realize everything begins with each individual."

Meanwhile in the midst of all the hard work and tight schedules, I was learning and growing in my personal life. In a letter to my family dated November 30, 1948, I wrote:

[Our group] is beginning to find new fellowship together, with trips together, walks and special suppers. We are getting to know each other and care for each other. Teamwork is the real thing of this life. Alone, I cannot do a thing in Germany.

I learned a few simple things these days: A quiet time every morning is absolutely essential, otherwise the whole day goes wrong and I miss many details . . . instead of dashing right and left doing many good things, I am beginning to learn to do the one inspired thing and then life is really fun—because all we are asked to do is to love God and do His will—that is not so difficult after all. In an insane world everything has been tried—why not try a new quality of life?

Following the war, a miner earned the equivalent of $3.00 a day. Comparatively, a good meal cost $1.00, a pound of coffee could be purchased for about $8.00, and a newspaper was $.04. As with the rest of Germany, housing was a major problem. Too many homes had been destroyed, and many refugees from the East had moved into this town.

The applause and enthusiasm expressed by the public at our shows was something almost forgotten in this town.

In a letter, I expressed what I saw in these German people:

It is a privilege to be in Germany and to serve Germany. Germany has done endless harm to the world, but if we keep blaming her, we would only create more division and more wars. By facing our own guilt, we also give hope to Germany. They seem to change and adapt faster than self-satisfied Americans like myself. Earlier, I came to Europe with the U.S. Army, but this experience is far greater than anything I ever thought possible. We are actually bringing hope to millions of people!

When the major German political party held their leadership meeting at Königswinter in late December, Dr. Adenauer, the chairman, asked us to perform *"The Forgotten Factor"*. Many party leaders were present. Later Dr.

Köhler, head of the Economic Council, was overheard saying that if the play should have been presented at the beginning of the conference, many unnecessary arguments would have been avoided. Other leaders expressed that they would like it performed in their states.

After the performance, we met some of Dr. Adenauer's children. The next day we received an invitation to have tea with the Adenauer family in Rhöndorf. Six of us from Britain, Germany and America spent a wonderful afternoon with the family in their lovely home above the Rhine River.

Seated around the Christmas tree we sang Christmas carols, shared our experiences, and told why we had left our homes to come to Germany at this time. As we were about to leave, Dr. Adenauer came in and we had a stimulating conversation with this leader who was later to become the first Chancellor of the Federal Republic of Germany. For over an hour he asked us questions. He wanted to know more about Caux and our experiences there. He took time to express his political philosophy and his vision for a united Europe.

This meeting was truly a highlight of my stay in Germany. Many people wait a lifetime to meet top political leaders. I felt most fortunate.

As we moved into the new year of 1949, I had time to reflect on how my life had changed. Four years earlier we had been fighting the Germans. Now British, French, Scandinavians, Germans and Americans were finding unity in working together. I considered what needed to be done to have the kind of world that was safe to live in, to enjoy our homes and our countries.

In early January we visited Bonn University. Most of the buildings had been destroyed and the books burned. For the 6,200 students, it was difficult to study. They listened to lectures in destroyed classrooms and slept in overcrowded quarters. A bunker—a former air raid shelter—was used for the main dormitory. Air pumps provided were placed underground in a mountain.

As we left the bunker one of our French friends commented that at least they had a place to sleep. In France, he said the students did not have even that.

We visited "Beethoven House," which had survived the war intact. This gave us a sense of the real values of the past and a sense of history. Another impressive sight was the "Münster," built around 700AD. It was only partly destroyed during the war.

A representative of the Bonn Student Council guided our tour through the University and through the city of Bonn. He had been a German officer. He seemed to be a very active young man. He told us that over Christmas he had visited his 73-year-old father who was teaching in the Russian occupied zone of Germany.

He described the terrible conditions. "When the Russians withdraw" he explained, "they will leave behind them a solid police state."

Only students who believed in class warfare were permitted to study. Workers and peasants were given priority. The communist party controlled the university, and indoctrination in Marxism was the basic aim of education.

The young man went on to explain that there was some resistance among the students, but since party members were the only ones allowed to study, this resistance was rapidly decreasing. People had become fearful and obedient. Under Hitler they had learned to obey, and since they went straight from Hitler to the Soviet control, they never tasted the freedom offered in the West. In the Soviet sector the cruelties of Buchenwald were not a thing of the past. People disappeared; there was no due process of the law. No one knew where they were taken, why they were taken, or if they would ever come back.

Our German friend expressed the hope that we still had time to alert Western Germany and Western Europe. He thought we still had time to prepare ourselves, so if we were taken over by the communists, we would know what to do.

He felt that many students in the West thought only of themselves. The young man felt the urgency to do something constructive and that is why he was active in student government. During the war he had been asked to join the resistance, he refused. Now, he openly admitted his guilt.

During this time, we spent much time with Dr. Adenauer's children, who were also students at Bonn University. They felt very privileged as they had kept many material things and survived the horrors of war almost unharmed—even though their father was a political prisoner at times. This I felt, was the most significant part of our being in Germany—our ability to meet young people and political and business leaders, not on an official basis, but as friends.

As the winter progressed, we were thankful for packages containing fruitcakes, chocolate, oranges, raisins, and even needles and thread sent by our stateside friends and families.

From reports of students who had come out of the Soviet Occupied Zone of Eastern Germany, we learned more and more about that zone. People were divided into three classes. Preference was given to "patriots" committed to class warfare, even former National Socialists who had accepted communism. Then there were the sons of workers and peasants. Finally, there were the academic youth. But since the other two classes were so numerous, most of the academic youth tried to escape to the West or forfeited their chance to study.

The most important requirement in Eastern Germany at that time was to be willing to fight the class war. Everything that comes in from the West was branded as Imperialistic/Capitalistic and was presented as totally negative.

In Leipzig the President of the Student Council belonged to a non-communist party. At the time of the elections the communist and the Soviet authorities attacked him and urged the students not to elect him. The workers and the trade unionists held a demonstration in front of the university. However, an overwhelming majority re-elected the student leader. Since their methods had failed, the communists had to use force. The student leader and ten others were arrested and charged with "conspiring against the Germans." The young student was condemned to twenty-five years of forced labor.

The methods used in Eastern Germany were similar to those of National Socialism. Buchenwald was repeated, but this time with no forced labor, no gas chambers, but a diet of complete silence. We are told it is more difficult to do absolutely nothing—have no books to read, no pencil and paper with which to write—to just be still.

Young people were being enlisted to become part of the secret police. One student from East Germany told us that a girl friend from his hometown visited Berlin. There she met American soldiers and had a nice conversation. When she returned home, she was accused of being in contact with the American secret service. She was then given the choice of being sent to Siberia or to enlisting in the Soviet Secret Service. This girl's father had been killed by the Russians; her mother lived with her and needed support. What could she do? She decided to work for the Russians. At first she did as little as possible, but living under constant fear of being sent to Siberia, she became one of Russia's spies.

We learned that the conditions in Eastern Germany were, for the most part, worse than in the West. A trip of four hours before the war now became a daylong venture. Railroad was functioning on one track.

In spite of pressures and dangers, we were told that the underground was still at work. The underground was like a chain; a member knew only the person ahead of him. In case of danger, he tried to inform two members. If they were also arrested, five people might be caught, but hardly more. Then the chain found a new link, and the work went on. The headquarters of this underground were in the American and British Zones. The work was even more effective than the resistance under Hitler.

The Soviets were very cruel, and often innocent people were arrested and put in jail simply because they had a friend in the West. Meanwhile, the youth were being increasingly indoctrinated with communist ideology, and we could see it would be difficult to bring anything new to Eastern Germany.

(Later, in 1961, the building of the wall ended any hope of effective change in Eastern Germany. The breathtaking event of the fall of the Berlin Wall on November 9, 1989, brought about the much needed change, followed by the unification of Germany in 1990.)

How then, we asked, can we help Eastern Germany? Our friends answered, "Bring unity to the West. Offer something better than communism."

It became increasingly apparent that if communism grew in Western Germany, Germany would be lost. If it succeeded in having a majority in France, France would be lost. The communists were working a well-devised plan. They used the democratic methods when it suited their needs. They encouraged the church, but in the proper time, would do away with it.

Our various friends kept telling us, "Give a better idea to the West—that is the only way to win the East."

That is exactly what we were trying to do. After our visit to the city of Bonn, we went back to Essen where we showed *The Forgotten Factor"* to miners, shop stewards and management. Among the crowd we had many members of the German Communist Party.

One evening after the show, we met a sixteen-year-old boy who told us this: "What is God? The priests hate me. I am honest with Dad, I never cheat at school, but the Christian children do. I am hungry in the mornings. I want to fight the capitalists. They have everything. Everybody ought to get what they deserve. Russia is bad, but much better than it has been. I study the Bible to learn to refute it. I am finding many loopholes! Christianity has been tried and failed. Marxism is not a Utopia, but it will come about. Hang the few who are responsible for the lack of food. Conditions needs to change, then all will be well."

What could we say to such a boy? His father was a leading communist and the boy was well trained. We talked with him, we had fun with him, and slowly he began to trust us, he even wanted to listen to his "inner voice."

This was his first written meditation: "American, Canadians, Russians, Germans, Capitalists and Communists all need change and bring change to others. It has to start with yourself."

This young fellow lost his hardness and became a person who really cared for his family. He brought his parents to see *"The Forgotten Factor"*. When they heard that Capitalists could change, they were amazed. This was a new dimension of human relations they had never heard before. Their daughter lost her bitterness as well and wanted to discover more about this new approach. The father then wanted to work with the socialist shop steward and with management to bring about change.

After our visit to the city of Essen, we went to Bochum, another mining community in the heart of the Ruhr. There the Executive Board of the Miners' Union saw *"The Forgotten Factor"*. The response was greater than ever. However, one prominent labor leader expressed himself, "If the occupation forces would leave, a capitalist would hang on every lamp post all the way down the street. There is plenty of hate and class war in this area."

According to Hubert Stein, one of the executives of the Miners' union, communists dominated 70 percent of the work councils in the Ruhr. Fortunately the labor youth responded favorably to our ideas. They wanted something better than class warfare. They seemed to understand the idea of change.

The National Union of University students invited us to participate at their meeting. The Student Council President of all German Universities was present. We listened to discussions of their social activities and their celebrations. Suddenly, we were asked to talk about our ideas, so we did. After we shared our ideas, the president of the Würzburg University Student Council said he had been searching for this idea for three years. He invited us to come to his university.

The chairman of the Hamburg University Student Council said he had learned of this idea earlier in Bonn and it changed his life. The student council of Hamburg University was working in a new spirit of "not *who* is right, but *what* is right."

As a result of this meeting, sixteen major universities invited us to come and bring *"The Forgotten Factor"* to their schools.

At one point we met Frau Teusch, the Minister of Education for North Rhine Westphalia. She sought our help and was highly interested in our program. After the interview with her, she introduced us to Dr. Arnold, one of the statesmen of Germany and Europe. When we visited with him in his home a few days later, he shared his ideas:

"Europe must be really united," he told us. "First it must be united spiritually, so out of it will come economic unity. Hitler destroyed a belief held by the German youth. Something new must come. A new living spirit can create

Europe. We need education and training. We need to acknowledge in Germany what personal freedom and responsibility for the State is. We must expect as much from the State as we expect from our family. This is the good road for Germany. The task of the statesman is to create ways to mobilize the best qualities in people. The negative forces will say 'What's that?' and then we will win the negative forces. The home is the cell of democracy, and from the home peace can spread to the nation and to the world."

The first few months in Germany were exciting. We gained insight into what was happening in both East and West Germany. We made many friends, hope arised in the hearts of the people—hope in the midst of a nation destroyed by war and defeat. But it was only the beginning.

John Pribram, George Adenauer, Gottfried Arnold, Fritz Heske, Jens Wilhemson
Picture of Whitsun 1950 "the Destiny for East and West"

CHAPTER 8
Democracy In the Ruhr

These faith-giving experiences in Germany began after World War II but continued through the fifties and into the early sixties. I had the opportunity to become acquainted with political, business, labor and youth leaders. With German delegations I visited other European countries and crossed the Atlantic a number of times to participate at International Conferences in America and to acquaint Germans with this great country of ours.

I was among those responsible for the distribution of a book by Peter Howard, *World Rebuilt*, to 120,000 German university students. The finances were raised through personal contributions and sacrificial giving by German students. The German government provided free mailing privileges for this undertaking. Major German universities invited us to follow up this campaign with seminars and conferences. Our aim was clear—to give hope to the German youth, to extend our welcome to them to become part of the youth of the world.

At Whitsun in 1950 the Communist Youth organized an international rally in East Berlin. At the same time, Moral Re-Armament organized a mass meeting in the Ruhr. We called it "The Destiny for East and West." We wanted to show that communists and non-communists, workers and mine managers and people from various countries could work together. And in fact, it was their destiny to do so.

Among the many speakers coming to the Ruhr for this special occasion was Mme Irene Laure, former Deputy in the French Chamber and Secretary General of the Socialist Women of France. Mme Laure was married to a Marxist. Her son had been tortured by the Nazis during the war. After giving reasons for her former hatreds, she extended the hand of friendship to a stunned and a most appreciative audience.

Also in attendance were George Adenauer, who brought a message from his father, Dr. Konrad Adenauer, Chancellor of the Federal Republic of Germany; and Gottfried Arnold, son of Dr. Karl Arnold, Minister-President of North Rhine Westphalia, who presented his convictions for the youth of Germany. Seated on the platform with these two young men were a former communist youth leader, a Norwegian resistance fighter, and myself. This type of fellowship demonstrated vividly the new spirit of understanding that was emerging in Europe.

The Ruhr minefields, which extend west of the Rhine as well as to the east, are some of the largest in the world. The area is a megalopolis–to leave one town is to arrive in another. Mine shafts dominate the landscape, along with vast areas of industrialization. We saw hundreds of identical houses crowded together–all looking alike. Then there would be miles of total destruction. Due to the bast amount of coal and iron available in the Ruhr, it has been said that whoever controls the Ruhr, controls Europe.

During my years in the Ruhr, I met many German miners. They had opposed Hitler's National Socialism. They had searched for an answer to Germany's problems and discovered a hope in communism. Some of them had spent the war in concentration camps. Those who survived reorganized the communist party after the war.

One of these was Hans Wessolek. Wessolek was chairman of his works council and his son was active in the "Free German Youth" the communist youth organization. Hans Wessolek had been a communist for thirty years and had been raised on a farm in utter poverty. While the owners of the large estate lived in luxury, his family barely survived. At Christmas sometimes the only gift he received was an orange, and that was very special.

Because of these experiences, Hans refused to accept a system where the few very rich dominated masses of the very poor. Class warfare seemed to be the only answer to the problems of his nation. It promised a better future for the workers of every nation.

I had never met a communist leader before, nor had I visited the home of a communist. I visited in the Wessolek home several times. He wanted to make us feel welcome, so he offered us Schnapps, the miners' drink, which we politely refused.

"Why don't you drink?" he asked us.

"We never take alcohol because we need clear heads for the task to which we are committed," we replied.

Our friend was surprised. As we visited, he took time to explain the ideas of dialectical materialism. He was convinced that change would come. He believed that history proved that finally the ultimate goal was being reached—a classless society.

I discovered in talking with Hans that communists are not different from us. Like us, they are filled with a passion to do something about the injustice and inequality in the world. But since their own personal needs have never been met, they believe the change of conditions alone will bring a solution to all their problems. And if one has not experienced "personal change," the only way to deal with difficult people is to eliminate them.

As our friend pulled out his cigarettes, he offered them to us. Again we refused. We explained that we needed all our resources for the task we had undertaken.

He was impressed and simply said that he too could stop smoking at any time.

A voice was heard from the kitchen. "Then why don't you stop?" It was Wessolek's wife.

We confronted Hans with new ideas. Hate only breeds hate. The extermination of one class may not necessarily lead to the happiness of the other class. Change certainly was needed, but on a monumental scale—change in the relations between nations, social and economic change to end poverty and despair. However, no change would become permanent unless based on personal change. Bitterness and despair needed to be replaced by love and understanding.

The "unknown" force some of us call "God" can work through our conscience and help us carry out our convictions, provided they are genuinely selfless.

Hans Wessolek talked with many of my friends, and he listened attentively. He was impressed that Norwegian resistance fighters, French survivors of concentration camps, American businessmen and many others had come to his country to help. He realized these were men who had every right to hate and even to turn their backs, but instead they had overcome these feelings..

Much later, he shared with me that he had listened to his "inner" voice and had only one thought. He had been a dictator as works council chairman, and yet he was opposed to dictatorship. To remedy this he apologized to his colleagues. It was very difficult. To his surprise he was re-elected as works council chairman, and a new spirit developed in the mine.

After listening to the inner voice a second time, he had a more difficult thought: "Get honest with your wife." To find courage for this, Hans said he prayed to the God to whom he had prayed as a child. That same God gave him the strength and courage he needed.

I had the privilege to accompany this communist leader as his interpreter on a trip to Great Britain. We visited the mines of Wales and talked to many workers, especially Marxists and communists. Everywhere Hans Wessolek went he shared the experience with a new way of life. He told of the unity he had found at home and at work and how it had affected the German coal fields.

Another miner, Hans Herrig, had been a member of the Communist Party for over twenty-five years. Herrig had a most unusual experience. One day he was working alone some 800 feet underground, digging out of the coal. Suddenly, he heard a voice, "Move quickly!"

As he obeyed, a large rock fell on the spot where he had been working.

"I could have been flattened like a postage stamp," this miner told us later. There in the mine he dropped to his knees and thanked God for saving his life. His life changed from that point. On his twenty-fifth wedding anniversary he asked the Bishop to perform a regular church wedding—something he and his wife had never experienced.

I accompanied Hans Herrig and his wife to the United States. I translated for him as he met miners in the coal fields of Pennsylvania and congressmen in Washington, D.C. He became a true ambassador for the new democracy developing in Western Germany.

The impact of the work in the Ruhr has been best expressed by a Norwegian student, Leif Hovelsen. Leif had been a resistance fighter during the war and was arrested by the Nazis at age nineteen. After the liberation, he discontinued his studies and his career and joined us in the work in the Ruhr. In his book, *"Out Of the Evil Night"*, Leif wrote:

"The communist functionaries and the miners who were drawn into the struggle were confronted with a simple moral choice. The issue was never a political one. It was the choice of whether or not they would commit themselves to the moral values and the truths that had been revealed to them through Moral Re-Armament or to follow in blind obedience to the Party line. They had to choose either to become free men under God, or remain exploited through the dictatorship of man.

Nowhere did such an ideological struggle rage as in the Nordstern Mine in Gelsenkirchen-Horst. In the communist battle to win the Ruhr, Nordstern was their chief stronghold. In 1946 a determined group of men decided to get control of the mine. They succeeded. In the works council, out of eleven members, ten were militant communists.

When "The Forgotten Factor" was presented in Gelsenkirchen in 1950, the miners were invited to see the drama. Miners from Britain came to meet the entire works council, to tell them what had been happening in the mines of Britain.

In November, a strike broke out in the mine. Two of the communists on the works council had been fired for provocative behavior. Less than thirty minutes later Radio Leipzig in the Russian Zone, was broadcasting the news, urg-

ing all the miners in the Ruhr to come out on strike in sympathy.

The works council itself sent strike committees around the Ruhr to get out all the 90,000 men of the Gelsenkirchen Coal Company, of which Nordstern is a part. The National Executive of the Miners' Union declared the strike illegal, but that made no difference to the communists. They were out to cripple the industrial life of the Ruhr.

The strikers' hope was not fulfilled. After three days the Nordstern miners returned to work. The plans for a sympathetic walkout came to nothing. What happened?

The manager of the Gelsenkirchen group of mines reported: 'There is just one reason why we were able to end the strike so quickly. The men in the responsible positions had become acquainted with the principles of Moral Re-Armament. That applies equally to employers, trade union officials, and the central works council of the company, irrespective of whether they were Socialists or Christian Democrats. That led to our finding of a common plan.'

I was told later by some of the men who had been involved in planning the strike that the strategy was to not only immobilize the German industry by it, but also to set off a wave of sympathetic strikes in France and in Italy.

News of this 'Greater Revolution' spread like wildfire. The ideas and the way of life embodied in the men took root in many parts of the Ruhr.

In the works council elections in 1949 and 1950, the communists had suffered a marked setback. This was made one of the chief subjects of discussions at the Communist Party Congress in Weimar on March 30, 1951.

'Such happenings have been related here,' said Party Boss, Walter Ulbricht. 'Show that our party has suffered such a setback in the works council elections in the mining industry in the Gelsenkirchen area of the Ruhr, that they should have been made the central point of the open discussions in the preparations for the Party Congress.'

The elections of 1951 marked the changing of the ideological trend in the Ruhr. The results of the 1953 elections were so remarkable that the Socialist Daily in the Ruhr, Westphalia Rundschau, used the headline, "Election Sensation!" Out of the new works council of the Nordstern mine, who had expanded to a total of twenty-three members, only four were communists.

If these men had fought a political battle alone, they would have soon dried up in their limited conceptions, and become framed in their own spheres of action. If they had only a personal experience of change, they soon would have found themselves self-satisfied with their garden and television sets. If their aim had been anti-communism, they would have joined the ranks of fearful *and bitter men, hard fighting, but without hope and vision of the future.*

These men found something far deeper, far more explosive. Grounded in the realism of their change, they had catapulted into God's space and vision for a New World in the making. Not always with an explicit understanding, the passion of Christ for a world gone astray, vibrated in their hearts."*

Approximately 200,000 people in twelve cities in Germany saw *"The Forgotten Factor"*, or *"The Good Road"*.

*"Out Of the Evil Night" by Leif Hovelsen, Blandford Press, London 1959

REPRINTED WITH PERMISSION BY THE AUTHOR.

CHAPTER 9
Berlin—The Divided City

I consider my visit to Berlin among my greatest experiences in Europe. I stayed there three and four weeks at a time, and I made many friends.

West Berlin is still one of the places where Americans are appreciated and liked by the population. The Berliner feels we have helped him to survive by giving him money, material goods, but even more—our hearts.

No wonder President John F. Kennedy had a tremendous response when, at a mass rally in Berlin, he identified himself with the city by saying, "Ich bin ein Berliner." ("I am a citizen of Berlin.")

At the time of the Berlin blockade in 1948, after the Soviets had closed the roads, the rails, and the canal that led to Berlin, the Allied Forces had mobilized an unprecedented force of air power. President Truman believe that saving Berlin was vital for the future of Europe. The full power of the United States and the British Air Forces was put behind the risky venture. Food, raw materials, and other essential supplies were sent to the beleaguered city. The city was saved from starvation, and West Berlin was saved from a Soviet takeover. This they would never forget.

When too many East Germans, especially young people, left their homes and moved to the West—or at least to West Berlin the communist authorities built a wall. It separated West Berlin from East Berlin, West Germany from East Germany.

To stand at the Berlin Wall was an unforgettable experience. Behind the wall on the communist side was a barbed wire fence. There were mine fields and watchtowers manned by the "Volkspolizei", the East Germany Communist police.

To escape from the East to the West became extremely difficult. Some tried to run across the field, while others tried to build tunnels. Most of the time they were chased by dogs and shot by their own countrymen! Very few survived.

To look across the wall into the East filled one with compassion for the millions who, not by their own choice but by force of events, were condemned to live under a ruthless dictatorship.

Berlin portrayed the reality of the world. In the West Germans experienced freedom, liberty, abundance of consumer goods, and a luxurious lifestyle. In the East there was Marxism, austerity, and a regimented lifestyle.

In 1953 there arose what was referred to as the "17th of June Uprising." Many citizens of East Germany rallied together and attempted to fight against communist control. This, of course, was quickly and forcibly quelled. One young man I met had been a leader of this uprising. This man had brazenly climbed up the Brandenburg Gate (one of Berlin's landmarks that separated East Berlin from West Berlin), and had torn down the communist flag. He then escaped to West Berlin.

At first he was considered a hero, but was soon forgotten. He became overwhelmed by "Western greed." He felt lonely and dejected, and at times questioned his wisdom in sacrificing his home and his future in the East to come to the West. As he became more familiar with our ideas of "practical" democracy, his outlook changed, and he discovered new ways he could contribute creatively to the reconstruction of the West.

Another student leader of Leipzig escaped to the West. He also accepted the need for change. He became obsessed with the idea of going back to his hometown in order to put things right with his own family and friends at the university. We were conscious of the dangers and tried to convince him to stay in the West. Unfortunately, we failed. The last we heard of him he had been accused of contacts with the American Secret Service. He was put in prison and condemned by the authorities to twenty-five years of forced labor.

West Berlin was often considered an island of democracy in the midst of the Red Sea. Fortunately our foreign policy throughout the years was committed to the freedom of West Berlin. Nowhere in the world was the reality of freedom vs. tyranny; life vs. death felt as strongly as in Berlin.

Once I was invited to accompany an American labor delegation on a visit to East Berlin. The American Embassy provided the cars. We passed Checkpoint Charley, the official American-Russian checkpoint, and drove along the main boulevard where very few people were walking in the streets and very few cars moving around. We visited the Gorky Museum. There, party officials explained to us the achievements of communism. As we moved around East Berlin, we saw very few happy faces. In fact, I felt as though we were constantly being watched. I was frightened throughout the visit. The entire party was relieved when we returned to West Berlin—to the free society to which all of us are so accustomed and yet often fail to appreciate.

On another visit to the border between East and West Germany, an East German policeman spotted our group from his watchtower. The closer we came, the more insecure he became. Finally, the policeman, who appeared to be very young, picked up his machine gun and pointed it at us, even though we were still on Western soil.

To his great surprise our group started to sing a song to him. It was a song about a united Germany, about a country where people care for one another.

The young policeman was stunned. He lowered and finally put aside his gun. As he listed, he seemed moved to tears.

On this and other occasions, we learned there is more than one way to *cross* the Iron Curtain.

November 9, 1989, the fall of the Berlin Wall became a most memorable day—a day of joy and freedom, the end of the Iron Curtain, and the beginning of a new relationship between East and West.

CHAPTER 10
Reconciliation Among Nations

For a number of years I worked with German political leaders. On occasion I accompanied parliamentary delegations to other countries. In 1952, I was invited to join two members of the German Parliament on a trip to Paris. It was their first visit to France, and they were fearful. They had served in the German Army on the Russian front. They had loved their country and wanted to fight for it. They had been fooled by Hitler, even though they had never joined the Nozi party. Now they had to identify themselves with their country's past and meet their French neighbors.

When the Germans were introduced to a large French audience, the atmosphere was icy. Then one of the Germans simply said, "You will never be able to forget what Germany has done to France, but please do forgive us. We want to rebuild Europe on a new basis of understanding and friendship." There was then a tremendous response.

Many similar interchanges between the French and the Germans developed into a new basis of trust. Chancellor Dr. Adenauer, Prime Minister Robert Schuman, and General Charles DeGaulle pioneered this new approach.

The significance of this new relationship between France and Germany needs to be seen in the perspective of history.

In 800 AD Charlemagne, kneeling before Pope Leo II, was crowned in Rome, "Emperor of the Romans." He had spent fifty years attempting to build a Christian Empire. He had united Western Europe except for Britain, Southern Italy, and the Mohammedan part of Spain.

After his death, Charlemagne's heirs quarreled. Civil War and disorder arose again. However, his three grandsons signed the "Treaty of Verdun" in 843. The Empire was divided into three separate kingdoms. Charles received the western part, roughly the size of France and Belgium; Louis, the eastern part that is present day Germany; and Lothar, the central part, Northern Italy, and Alsace-Lorraine.

Lothar died soon after the signing of the treaty. His kingdom became the battleground between Charles and Louis. For generations to come each side claimed control of the Middle Kingdom. Countless wars were fought for over one thousand years.

Brother against brother turned into a struggle of nation against nation.

Before 1871 Alsace-Lorraine belonged to France. After the Prussian-French war became part of Germany. After World War I it became French again. During World War II Germany made it part of the Third Reich, and now it is French again.

Throughout history bitterness, hatred and revenge became deeply ingrained in the hearts of the French and the Germans. History textbooks supporting nationalism influenced millions of people.

When I first visited France and Germany after World War II, reconciliation between those two nations seemed possible.

Today, thanks to many courageous people, friendship between those two great European nations is a reality.

A very good friend of mine, Engelbert Heller lived in East Germany. There his father was active in politics before Hitler took over Germany. After the war, he was one of the founders of the Christian Democratic Party in the Soviet Zone of Germany. My friend fought with the German armies against Russia, was captured, and spent many years in Russian prison camps. When he was finally released, he discovered that his parents had been mistreated by the Russians, and his homeland had been occupied by the conquerors. In 1950 he succeeded in escaping from the Soviet Zone to the West where he decided to study theology and become a priest.

When I met Engelbert, he represented the students on the Bonn University Student Council. He wholeheartedly accepted the ideas we stood for. According to him, it was "true Christianity." He made the decision to apologize to one of his professors, after which he returned several books to the library that he had considered his own. A number of other students followed his lead. They were attacked by all those who refused to accept this challenge of absolute honesty followed by restitution.

Later, as a priest, Engelbert had weekly meetings in his home with other priests. Although he did not personally smoke or drink, he served wine, beer and cigars. During one of these meetings some of his young people visited him. They were already in trouble because of extensive use of liquor and tobacco. Only after this, the priest chose to begin serving coffee and cake to his fellow priests was he able to give the help needed to these young people. His parish became a dynamic center of new life.

His selfless dedication to workers, to the elderly, but especially to young people had a profound impact. I was privileged to accompany Engelbert on visits to England, where he spoke about his own country and also shared his personal experiences at various assemblies. He visited France, Belgium,

Holland, Denmark and Norway which had been at odds with Germany in the past. He traveled with the international force of "Up With People" to Brazil and he came to the United States. Wherever he went, he built bridges between people of his nation and other nations.

After World War II Germany became a place of refuge for millions of people who did not want to live under communist occupation. Refugee camps sprang up all over Germany. East Europeans filled many camps in Bavaria.

The Minister of Refugees for Bavaria invited us to visit a camp called "Válka," which translated into English meant "War." Here Czechs, Slovaks, Ukrainians, and Cossacks were crowded into Army barracks. Most of these people had escaped communist domination in their own countries, and refugee camps were the only way the government had to deal with them. There was nothing for the refugees to do but sit and wait for something to eat each morning and again each night and hope that they would get out someday. The refugees were filled with utter hopelessness.

Having been a refugee myself, I knew the first thing a refugee does is question, "Why am I where I am?" Next, he blames those whom he feels are at fault. Quickly the refugees at Válka had created political factions, each blaming the other for the communist takeover of their countries. In the cover of night, knife fights were a common occurrence.

This camp was almost considered off-limits for a non-refugee to enter, and it was a dangerous undertaking to visit this camp.

However, we wanted to bring hope to those who had lost their homes, their jobs and their countires.

I was responsible for the meeting with all the refugees. The program consisted of speakers from many nations and an international chorus. We started with a song in the Czech language. Suddenly a refugee rushed forward, he wanted to speak.

I was hesitant for fear he would disrupt the meeting and attack the minister of refugees who was present among the dignitaries. It was possible our efforts would fail completely. Reluctantly, I gave him permission.

To my great surprise, the refugee gave us flowers and thanked us for coming to the camp. He expressed his gratitude for the people who cared enough to come to the camp and bring hope to the refugees.

Countless experiences, like the few I have mentioned, in refugee camps, in the industrial areas of Germany, in politics and among the young helped in laying the foundation for democracy in Germany and establish new relationships between Germany and her various neighbors.

PART III:
Education, Tomorrow's Hope

"Sing-Out", Deutschland, 1968

CHAPTER 11
Up With People

In 1965 a new initiative developed among American youth. A musical called, "Sing-Out" was produced. Later the name was changed to *Up With People*.

According to the *Tulsa World*, October 9, 1983:

Up With People *is an educational and cultural organization seeking to give young people a learning experience that develops global awareness, sensitivity to others, and self-reliance to build bridges of understanding and communication among people, cultures, and countries, utilizing original musical productions in pursuing these aims.*

It offers its members learning opportunities in fields such as stage production, public relations, business and personnel management, and cross-cultural education. Since it became an independent, educational corporation, over 7,000 students have participated in the program.

The group's show is performed by five casts with 125 students each who give more than 600 annual performances. Its members are ages eighteen through twenty-six and come from eighteen different countries. It has performed for eight million people in forty-seven countries.

By 1989, over ten thousand young people had participated with *Up With People*.

I had the privilege to participate at the Silver Reunion of the *Up With People* Alumni Association in Denver in July 1990, where Blanton Belk, founder and president of *Up With People* said:

In 1990 we were able to realize a long time dream of having Soviet Youth participate in our program. One hundred Soviet students are joining the casts. These young Soviets are an exciting addition to one of our most successful recruiting years in our history in terms of cultural diversity. For the first time, we have representatives from every continent at the same time and working together for a common future.

Dr. Morris Martin in his book "Born to Live In the Future" describes *Up With People*'s mission as of May 1990:

To build understanding among nations and to spark people to action in meeting the needs of their communities, countries and the world; and to equip young people with leadership qualities of global perspective, integrity and motivation to service. * *See Appendix "Friendship Renewed at Anniversary"

Back in 1966, at the time of the first performances of *Up With People,* relations between the United States and the Federal Republic of Germany had reached a dangerous low. Chancellor Ludwig Ehrhard decided to show Germany the "real" America and invited *Up With People* to tour Germany. The German response to the American youth was unbelievable. They wanted to become part of the international movement of understanding.

To help the teenagers in this new adventure, a traveling high school was created in Germany. In this school I was asked to teach history, government, and French.

Teaching history in a school based in Germany revealed various interesting aspects. Students from Northern Germany had been taught the significance of Martin Luther and the Reformation. Protestants brought freedom of religion to their oppressed lands, Catholicism was attacked as authoritarian.

Students from Southern Germany, especially from Bavaria, based their history on close ties with the Roman Catholic Church. Martin Luther was almost ignored in their textbooks. Ignatius of Loyola's Reformation of the Catholic Church was the most significant event for Germany at that time.

Students who had escaped from the East came indoctrinated with the concept of class warfare. They had studied the importance of workers and peasants throughout history. These students knew nothing about the more recent history because they had had teachers who feared to mention National Socialism.

I tried to draw out the best the students had learned so far and develop an objective approach to history, where everyone, regardless of class, race or religion could play a constructive part.

The young people created a musical program, similar to *Up With People.* It was taken across Germany to the neighboring countries of France, Denmark, Norway, Austria, Switzerland, and Italy. It showed a determination of this new generation to leave the past behind and to work together for the future.

In the spring of 1967 Brazil invited this group of 150 youth from many nations to present this program, I accompanied them. We visited Rio, Sao Paulo, Blumenau and many other cities. We stayed in the homes of the well-to-do, and we saw the "pavelas" where the poorest of the poor barely exist.

The highlight of our visit was in Brazilia. The Brazilian Air Force flew us into the city. However, the students were demonstrating against us. "Yankee go home." We did not know whether we would be able to have a performance of *Up With People.* The students of the Medical Faculty invited us to a meeting. It was to be an open protest against Yankee Imperialism.

Fortunately, a delightful young black American singer named Pat Ector had joined our European group. Before singing the song, "What Color Is God's Skin," Pat talked to the demonstrating crowd.

"We know you hate America," she said. "We have made many mistakes in the past. Please forgive us. We are here because we want to build a better world, and we want to do it with you."

The atmosphere changed. *Up With People* was played to overcrowded audiences. Our visit to Brazil was a most worthwhile undertaking.

While I was traveling with the Up With People High School through Germany, I had a very important personal experience. It was simple, yet had far-reaching affects for my life. During my morning meditations on New Year's Day, 1968, while searching for God's plan for the situation I was in, I had a startling thought: "Ask the nurse traveling with the high school to marry you."

It certainly seemed a very unusual thought coming out of the blue! I knew the lady, Agnete Husfeldt, who was from Denmark. Agnete was not only the nurse for the 150 young people, but also a counselor and a true friend. Sometimes I had transported her patients in my car. I had come to know her well and I liked her. But to marry her was certainly an unusual thought! But the more I thought about her, the more I experienced a deep love for her.

I wrestled with this thought just as I had wrestled with other thoughts during my life. Of course, I was filled with fears—fears she would say no, fear I would get hurt, and fear I would not be able to provide adequately for my wife.

However, I had also learned to accept that "fears are liars" and only with a clear head, free from emotions, could a right decision be made.

I became increasingly convinced that it was God's amazing plan unfolding for me and my Danish friend. I talked it over with some of my best friends. They encouraged me to move ahead and propose to her. In order to give her time to think, I wrote her a letter. I was convinced she would accept this marriage proposal the same day.

The young people were getting ready to leave for Italy and Scandinavia and Agnete was kept busy the entire day vaccinating the cast members.

Still convinced my proposal would be answered the same day, but tired from the long wait, I went to bed early. At 10:30 p.m. a friend of mine knocked at my door, asking me to get dressed quickly. The young lady, Agnete, wanted to see me!

She had read my letter in the morning, but since she had much work to do, she decided to wait until nightfall to think about it. Then in prayer, it became clear to her to say "yes" that same evening. It was the best thing that ever happened to me. Both of us felt it was God's amazing plan. We were meant to share our lives with each other and pass on many experiences we had had. The best years of our lives lay ahead of us.

Before we were married, Agnete had been asked to join the U.S. cast of *Up With People.* I took advantage of one of the international conferences to come to the states to see her. For a short time I traveled with this group on the East Coast. The Superintendent of Education for *Up With People* talked with me about helping to develop the traveling school in the United States. I gladly accepted this invitation.

Once again I was at the end of one era in my life and on the brink of another.

We were married in Copenhagen. It was truly an international wedding. The Dean of the Cathedral of Copenhagen performed the ceremony.

My brother Otto, then American Military Attaché in Bulgaria, was best man.

John and Agnete Pribram
Wedding in Copenhagen, November 9, 1968

Agnete's father, Erik Husfeldt, a well-known heart surgeon, president of the Danish Red Cross and one of the leaders in the Danish Resistance Movement, gave away the bride. A delightful German couple, very close friends of ours, was part of the family wedding party.

Messages came from friends in Germany, among them members of par-liament, industrialists, former communist leaders, the children of Dr. Adenauer, the vice-Mayor of Berlin, and the cast of *Up With People* in Europe. Messages were also sent by friends in France, among them the family that had taken care of me when I was a young refugee escaping from the invading Germans. Other messages came from Great Britain, Belgium, Switzerland, Finland, Norway, Sweden, of course from Denmark, and the *Up With People* cast per-forming in the United States.

It was an unforgettable experience for my new bride and me. It portrayed to everyone that a new world, free from prejudices of the past, was emerging through the hearts and minds of countless people. *

From then on Agnete and I worked together with the same commitment. Through *Up With People* we were responsible for hundreds of young people, my wife as nurse for the cast and I as vice-principal and social studies teacher of the Up With People High School.

The pace for the students and staff was a hectic one. In the mornings the students were brought in from the homes where they were staying to another area pre-designated as their makeshift school. It may have been in a church, extra rooms in a school, a multi-purpose community building, or even a library. We conducted a cast meeting to make certain each person was comfortable in his or her host home. At this time members were briefed on the day's up-coming events as well as rehearsal announcements.

From there the students spent four hours in class time. Often, lunch was pro-vided by the community and then back to class again. By late afternoon rehearsals were started, and it was not uncommon to see students off-stage doing their homework, waiting to be called.

Dinner may have been provided by the Rotary or some such organization, or a student may have been invited back to the host home for dinner. In the evening, of course, was the presentation of the show and following that, time to talk with community young people who might be interested in joining the cast.

Late at night the students were taken back to the homes, where there may have been another couple hours of conversation with the hosts before finally getting to bed.

*See Appendix "Letter from Germany after Re-unification"

In each community students were offered the opportunity to meet key people. They sat in on meetings of city commissions, or met the mayor, or toured a historical point in the area. We attempted as much as possible to make their education practical. For instance, if a student was going to write a paper on urban development, from city to city, he could gather information for his paper.

In one unit, we studied the Native Americans, so for a time in each community, we were contacting Native Americans from the various tribes who were available to come and speak to the students.

The students traveled in several large Greyhound buses. Agnete and I followed in our Volkswagen station wagon, a gift from some friends in Europe. This was a great help when at times we needed to carry sick students in our car.

The students in the *Up With People* High School were from different parts of the United States and from different ethnic and socio-economic backgrounds. They had seen the performance and were inspired by the production. Each one was required to apply to the high school and then be accepted.

To travel with the cast, some financial resources were needed. Some students earned the needed money. Others emptied savings accounts or talked to civic clubs in their communities.

Lila came from Florida. She had never left home before joining *Up With People*. She had lived a sheltered life in an upper middle class home. Lila had never really met young people from other ethnic backgrounds and never had an opportunity to talk with them.

On one of our social studies field trips we visited the slums of a city. Lila had never seen such proverty. She couldn't believe people would have to live in such shacks. She was disturbed, appalled and didn't quite know how to cope with such injustice.

As Lila became more familiar with other young people, she said, "This type of education experience has opened me up to learn about things I know nothing about, share the things I do know, and listen to what other people are saying."

Julia, elected as Miss Black Teenage Rochester, participant in a Miss Black Teenage USA pageant, was attracted by the vibrance and wholeheartedness of *Up With People*. Her father, a meatpacker, graciously gave permission for his daughter to study in the high school. She had a charming personality and was an excellent singer.

As we visited a small town in Missouri, one of Julia's friends stayed at home, scared to go out after dark. In that community they had "Blue Laws." A black that was found on the streets after dark could be arrested and sent to jail. Since there were no black residents in that community, the law was never repealed.

Julia reacted differently to this serious problem of racial prejudice. One day, when ordering a meal in a restaurant, the waiter approached Julia and said, "We don't serve blacks."

Julia looked at him and replied, "That's all right. I would like chicken."

Julia had a great sense of humor and had overcome hurts due to her race, and was proud of her heritage. She helped us to understand what it meant to be black in a country where prejudice is still very deep. During the performances when she sang, "What Color Is God's Skin?" She helped hundreds of people to reach the conclusion—"It is not a question of color, but of character."

"What I experienced earlier," Julia said, "was just studying to get an "A" on the test. But in this high school they told me I had to be responsible for my education. I found that the only way to educate myself was to get out and use every source, every ability I have in me in order to make the best product I can. Education became not so much a nine to three venture, but a life venture."

During our stay in Tahlequah, Oklahoma, several of the cast members roomed with Indian students of the Sequoyah High School. Linda, a Cherokee senior and the elected "Miss Sequoyah", was granted a full scholarship to travel with *Up With People* by the Cherokee Nation.

Linda came from a humble home in Oklahoma. She proudly represented the native Indian heritage in our cast. Every night on stage, she said a prayer in sign language to the "Great Spirit."

Linda invited us to meet her family—many brothers and sisters, nieces and nephews, aunts and uncles. We felt almost adopted by the Cherokee Tribe. We saw the "Trail of Tears," a Cherokee production of the agony of the Indians when, some 150 years ago, they were forced to leave their homelands and move to Indian Territory. On the 600-mile journey, many died in the bitter cold. The sufferings they endured were told to their children and their grandchildren.

Lila, Julia and Linda became great friends. They came to know one another and discovered that basically they were the same. Prejudice could be overcome, because each of them wanted to be part of a new generation building a world that works.

As their social studies teacher I became the facilitator. Linda taught us of the Native American heritage. Julia made the black experience come alive for us, and Lila represented the cross section of Americans who never realized the great contribution other ethnic groups had made in shaping this nation.

I was privileged to know these young people. My Harvard education never gave me this deep insight in the three major cultures of our society.

Up With People also provided us with a unique opportunity to get to know the United States by living in our countless homes across the country.

One time we were invited to stay with the leader of a Mexican community. His home was in the slum area of the town. His sons came in the pickup truck to meet us upon arrival. At their home we were put in the garage which had been transformed into a bedroom. It was a very cold night. In the morning it took quite a while to share the one bathroom used by the family of eight. Everyone in this home was extremely outgoing. We were treated as their most welcomed guests. They shared their meals with us and made us feel at home.

At the other end of the spectrum, we stayed in a mansion at Palm Springs. The bathroom was as large as the entire home of our Mexican friends. There was a golf course in the "back yard."

For a few weeks, we stayed with a dentist and became part of his family. On Thanksgiving Day we discovered that the dinner, so lovingly prepared for this large family, was not as important as the Oklahoma-Nebraska football game, when all the men left the table to gather in front of the television set.

In Nevada we stayed with a teacher. We shared our experiences and ideas about education. When we returned the following year, we were invited to stay with him again.

In Kansas we stayed with a square-dancing champion and in Oklahoma with a barber and a lawyer. In Arizona we were in the guesthouse of a rancher. Unfortunately, a skunk had made its home there as well. It took a number of days for our clothes to recover from this unique experience.

At Lake Havasu in Arizona we were the first to cross the London Bridge, bought and transported stone by stone from London.

In Arizona we experienced tropical weather in February and in Canada snow at the end of May.

We crisscrossed the United States receiving a warmhearted welcome and becoming a part of each community. Driving by car and by bus, we became conscious of this great continent. In the West we could drive for hours without seeing any homes, and in the East it was like a megalopolis.

Everywhere we went we met people who cared and wanted to play their part in creating a better world.

After five years on the road with *Up With People*, first in Europe and then through Canada and at least thirty states in the United States, Agnete and I decided it was time to stop living out of a suitcase. We settled down and made our home in Tulsa, Oklahoma, where the Monte Cassino School offered me a job as social studies teacher. Now came the opportunity to put into practice in a stationary position the many experiences learned on the road. And yet another phase of my life was beginning.

John with Mr. Ernst Reinecke from Germany, Mr. & Mrs. Toyo Sohma, Educators from Japan and Ms. Inger Hansen, Educator from Denmark at the *Up With People* Alumni Reunion.

John and Agnete with Constance Newman at the *Up With People* Alumni Silver Reunion in Denver, CO, July 1990.

CHAPTER 12
Social Studies: Preparation For Life

At a time when education has become one of the major issues in this country, when the quality of the educator is questioned and when it seems so important to raise the SAT and ACT scores, I believe it is time to take a fresh look.

Education, including the high school level, is very much in need of radical change, If it is to meet the challenges of our age. Most teachers still believe in a traditional approach. Recently, for example, at the Oklahoma State Convention for Social Studies Teachers, a teacher told about show a special film in her class. Later she learned that her students had seen the same film in an English class and had discussed the same subject in Biology. No wonder student get bored and turned off.

Unimaginative and uninspired ways are only too common in my field of teaching. Why does a history teacher talk about Lincoln in January? Because that's the time planned for the Civil War. Why doesn't he talk about President Bush? Because he used the traditional chronological approach and never gets to the present. Why is there so little study of Black History? Because our textbooks have been written by white people. Why do we talk about the Chinese living in the Far East? Because years ago we decided that longitude 0° should run through Greenwich, England. From there we move to Western Europe, Eastern Europe, Middle East and Far East. Yet for the Chinese, China has been and is the "Middle Kingdom" and center of the universe.

Fortunately, there has been a growing trend among social studies educators to get away from the traditional and to encourage the "Inquiry approach," to develop critical thinking and also learn through field trips and other methods.

I was privileged in my work with the *Up With People* High School in the United States and Europe, to find myself in the midst of these and other innovations. As I developed the school's social studies program, I was able to experiment and learn with other educators how best to use our resources. We discovered, of course, the best resource was the people we were meeting, whether in Rome, Rio, or Bonn, whether in parliament, Army camp or factory.

A student who had the privilege to travel with *Up With People* gained a world perspective, an appreciation and a better understanding of his fellowman. He worked together with black, white and yellow to overcome the many prejudices that has separated them for centuries.

True education about Europe, for example, is better found in Europe, in European families, than in textbooks that are sometimes not even up to date.

True initiative is gained when a student takes on a task way beyond himself, as do the students who have to prepare for the coming of the cast to a community. They work with the leaders to find board and room and to publicize the show. They discover more about city government in one day than in weeks of classroom study.

Up With People students have the opportunity to discover their true calling –in politics, business, public relations, or other professions whether or not they start with good incentives, by the time they leave the traveling program, they are usually highly motivated to play their part in their own community.

All these developments are in the forefront of the changes that are beginning to take place in high school education. Many of them can be applied to a stationary situation, whether it is the approach of treating students as young adults, or field trips to city hall, discussions with guest speakers, conferences with students about their grades, or encouraging them to get involved in community projects.

When I left *Up With People*, I joined the staff of Monte Cassino, a private school in Tulsa, Oklahoma. At the time, Monte Cassino had been in the process of implementing many of the same ideas I had been learning and trying out on the road with the cast.

For twelve years, I headed Monte Cassino's Social Studies department where the headmaster wholeheartedly encouraged me in developing an innovative curriculum.

One of my most interesting courses, for example, was Government in Action given to tenth grade students in January. The magazine, Social Studies Professional in its March 1972 issue, briefly summarized the course as among the fifteen "promising practices" of innovative education in the United States. As a result of this brief summary, I received letters from almost every state in the United States and from Canada and Australia. Teachers, supervisors and school board members wanted to know more about the course.

Then in January 1973, the course was improved. To my great surprise two of the students participated at the Scholastic Competition for high school students of Oklahoma at Central State University and won gold and silver medals in civics.

After that, the students placed among the first four, winning gold and silver medals most of the time. In 1982 the Oklahoma State Department of Education included an outline of the course as part of <u>Classroom Learning Activities for Social Studies.</u>

This course was successful because the students had the opportunity to experience "government in action," at City Hall, the Oklahoma Legislature, at court trials, and at the Juvenile Delinquency Center. They met political leaders, talked to city officials, police officers and lawyers and conducted their own mock trials. The practical knowledge gained through field trips was supplemented with research projects and resource material, especially the American Constitution.

Every course I taught began with the question, "What do you want to learn?" Often an outline for the coming weeks developed out of the first discussion. One year teaching World Issues, the oil crisis was the major problem. The father of one of the students, just back from oil negotiations in Venezuela, talked to the class. At the time of the Iranian crisis students from Iran, some still favoring the Shah and others for the Ayatollah Khomeini debated the issue.

More recently nuclear issues overshadowed the international scene. The father of one of the students, just back from a visit to the Strategic Military Command in Omaha, Nebraska, filled us in on the latest.

When the stock market created some concern, an expert explained its inner workings to the class.

The World Issues class developed a model United Nations Security Council, where each student became responsible for a country represented at the United Nations Security Council in New York. After weeks of preparation, with helpful material sent to inquiring students by the respective United Nations Embassy, resolutions were drafted and current issues discussed.

This approach was so stimulating, that the students helped to create a model United Nations for the Tulsa high schools. Twice they raised enough money for a Tulsa delegation to participate at the model United Nations Assembly in New York City.

In the course of United States history, when we were studying the 1933 depression, one student's mother, a professor of economics at Tulsa University, came to help us to understand its ramifications.

A leading black educator explained to the students what is meant by "black experience" and recalled her days at the University of Oklahoma when she was not permitted to sit in the same classroom with other students or eat in the cafeteria.

Black leaders of Tulsa also invited a number of students to a luncheon at which Pat Latimer, Up With People High School graduate, spoke about her election as first black female student council president at Oklahoma State University. For most of my students, as whites, this was their first experience in such surroundings.

Native American speakers helped us to understand and to appreciate the rich Indian heritage.

The basic belief underlying these activities is one very familiar to any student or teacher in the *Up With People* program. Education is not only what happens inside the four walls of the classroom, more importantly, it concerns the entire life of the individual. True learning is not a monopoly of the teacher, but of all of us searching for a deeper understanding of this world. The purpose of social studies is a sincere concern for the future, an attempt to live in the present and to keep learning from the past in order to better understand the present and become more prepared for the space age in which we live.

In order to do this, the responsibility of education is placed more and more in the hands of the learner. Facts and dates may be important, but even more important is the ability to know where to find them.

Every year after the first quarter, students had to evaluate the course they were taking with me. They were asked to give their ideas of how to improve it, and thus develop with me the work for the second quarter. I adopted the same approach to grades. The students wrote out their own evaluation of their work and the grade they thought they deserved. Then we had a one-on-one conference, and we decided together the grade the student would receive. This developed an excellent way of communicating with the student. Most of the time they graded themselves the same way I did.

In all classes the students worked on a project of their choice. Thus, they had an opportunity to do research and read about something that was of genuine interest to them. Then they shared their findings with the rest of the class. This was usually followed by lively discussions. Recently, one student took the side of Israel and another the side of PLO. The students not involved in the debate were the jury and judged the arguments.

There were other responsibilities for which my earlier experiences prepared me. As sponsor of the Student Council, of the National Honor Society and Dean of Studies, I had the opportunity to be in constant contact with the activities of the students. Most important is the way we treated them. We tried to deal with them as young adults and to be open-minded and learn from them as we moved along. It was a two-way process.

As Dean of Studies I was responsible for the student's curriculum, helping the weaker students and challenging the more gifted ones, and sometimes dealing with problems concerning students, faculty, and parents.

Part of my teaching assignment was to be director of independent studies. We did not offer some courses like the History of Great Britain, Russian History or Economics, but a student could pick such subjects, confer with me once a week, and work on his own the rest of the week. This gave the student a pre-college experience and increased his motivation. Whether a student was learning more about Communism or about Africa, the one who gained the most was the instructor. I learned new things everyday.

Community involvement was another very important part of our education program. Students participated in such projects as UNICEF, Food for the Needy, Save the Trees Campaign, Vision 2000 (a program in which young adults plan with the Tulsa City Commission for the year 2000), Tulsa Youth Forum, and so on.

Each January for a number of years, juniors and seniors had the opportunity to try out careers, such as working one month in a hospital, the mayor's office, or a lawyer's office.

These activities simply underline a few basic convictions that have come to guide me as an educator:

First, *the student's education is all of life. It is not to prepare him for some distant future, but he can start right now. He can participate in a career of his choice while still in high school.*

Second, *the most important and most difficult element in education is motivation. The teacher's task is to be a stimulator or an activator. Once in a while a student will find his life's calling—to help needy children, to become a doctor, or to enter politics.*

Finally, *an equally important part of high school education is showing young men and women how to get along with people and how to create a society with less prejudice and more understanding of each other, of other races and other cultures. Then mankind may not only survive, but also shape a creative future.*

In a letter to the Valley Forge Freedom Foundation, former Tulsa Mayor Jim Inhofe (now U.S. Senator Inhofe) said this of my teaching:

"I am well acquainted with Mr. Pribram and the great contribution that he has made to the young people of the City of Tulsa in terms of instilling in them the importance of freedom in our society . . . Each year he would bring all his students to City Hall in order to expose them to the actual workings of government on a day to day basis. I am also aware that he did the same with

other levels of government. In fact, I used to assist him when I was a member of the State legislature when he would bring groups to Oklahoma City . . . There is no one in Tulsa that is more aware of the importance of maintaining a free society and his life is a testimony of that."

For twelve years I was chairman of the Social Studies Department at Monte Cassino. At an awards assembly I thanked the faculty and the students, informing them I would not be returning the next year. To show their love and appreciation, students and faculty gave me a standing ovation. The Monte Cassino faculty presented me with an award for "twelve years of dedicated teaching."

At the traditional class night, when the seniors made fun of their friends and of the faculty, the president of the National Honor Society, the president of the senior class and the president of the Pep Club thanked me by giving me balloons with special inscriptions of appreciation.

"No class has had as much influence on me as the World Issues class," one note read, "and no teacher has had as much influence on me either."

History to most students is thought to be boring and a waste of time. But these messages from my former students contradict that notion. One of my more difficult students, who at first showed little interest in history, approached me the last day of school and said, "In the name of the next year's senior class I want to ask you to reconsider your decision and stay for another year."

Another note read: "Just about everything I know about history, and I am being sincere, is due to your classes. Thank you for your confidence and support."

"Thanks for a great year in history, I really love this class, I mean it!" said another.

Yet another student scribbled this at the end of her final exam: "Thanks Mr. Pribram, we will miss you—now we know the world inside out. You are a *great* friend!"

Parents as well came to me with thanks and appreciation. This response was most rewarding. The students and staff at Monte Cassino made this time in my life a worthwhile experience.

From Monte Cassino, I moved to Union Junior High School, still in Tulsa. It is one of the best public schools in this region. Administration, teachers and parents work together to give the very best to the 1,300 students. Half of them are in the 8th grade, the other half are freshmen. The school has an excellent curriculum including foreign languages, debate, creative writing and special academic competition as well as a very elaborate music program.

For the last eight years I have been teaching American and Oklahoma History to freshmen, and Civics to eighth graders. It has been a most enjoyable experience. *

Every year I start my classes with this question. "What will you be doing in the year 2010? Will you have a family? What will the world be like some twenty years from now?"

My students answered this question recently with some very interesting results. Some students expected to have large families and live in beautiful homes somewhere in California or in Florida. Others expected to be teachers, nurses, doctors, lawyers, or car mechanics. Working with computers was high on the list. Some wanted to go out for professional football or baseball; one planned to become the number one tennis player, and another intended to be the first woman president of the USA.

The world is expected to be at peace, robots will be widely used in homes, with flying cars for everyone. There will be interplanetary travel and one student expected to live on a space station. Only two students predicted World War III and total destruction. Hope and much to live for typified the all-around feeling of the students.

As the students examined their heritage, they discovered that most of them were American citizens. There were a few exceptions, a few Vietnamese, some Korean and a student from Lebanon. Most of their ancestors came from Europe, especially from Germany, England, and Ireland. There were a few students whose ancestors came from Africa, and of course there were a number of Native Americans.

Very few students have lived in just one home all their lives, or were born in Tulsa. This demonstrated the tremendous mobility within our country. Most of the students came from middle class homes, few were very rich, and few were very poor. Some came from two-parent families, but there were quite a number of students coming from broken homes.

This proved to be a good way to get to know the students and develop one's teaching accordingly.

An article published in <u>Today's Catholic Teacher,</u> Peter Li, Inc., reprinted with permission of publisher, Dayton, Ohio, April 1989 "A Living Civics Course" best summarizes my experiences at the Union Junior High School.

Civic class had a new look last year for a Tulsa (OK) junior high class. Through a series of presentations, role-playing activities, and practical experiences, eighth graders developed both their political and their economic IQs.

*See Appendix "A letter from Principal Larry Elliott"

In a study of government, it is important that students discover why we created the kind of government we have and why we strive for a prejudice-free world.

A film by a third-grade teacher caught the attention of the class. In it, brown-eyed people are considered more talented than blue-eyed people are. They are praised, given special privileges, and encouraged to persecute blue-eyed people. Then the process is reversed, with the blue-eyed people in control.

Seeing this film helped the students better understand the protections built in by our Constitution, particularly the Bill of Rights. As part of the study of the Constitution, the class developed its own constitution, the preamble of which was "to create a more perfect Union" (our school's name, incidentally).

The class became a legislative assembly, electing its own officers and determining the terms of each. Terms were set at just one month to allow more students to hold office. Because they wanted to have money for a class party, they needed a treasurer. Bills were proposed, a few of which were enacted into law: e.g. "If a student fails to have a book cover, or forgets his/her textbook, or disturbs the class, he or she will have to pay a fine of ten cents or copy a page from the civics book."

A state representative was invited to explain our legislative system. He discussed what it would take to drop the driving age to fourteen, as some young people would like. His explanation helped the students understand why it would be better to raise the age to eighteen, rather than keep it at sixteen.

The class enjoyed seeing "Animal Farm." It helped them understand why government is necessary and why a democracy is preferable to a dictatorship.

Study of our judicial system included visits by a district attorney, father of one of the students, and a lawyer, father of another. They explained the differences between civil and criminal cases, choosing of a jury, and the procedure in a trial. A video about the famous Gideon case explained the Supreme Court decision that every accused person has the right to have a lawyer.

The opportunity arose to put these understandings to work. Two students were thirty seconds tardy for class. Instead of sending them to the office, we held a trial. The students picked their own defense lawyers. A district attorney, a judge, and a bailiff were chosen from the class. There were various witnesses, and the rest of the class made up the jury. The classroom became the courtroom. As the trial proceeded, even two students from another class were permitted to testify as to the character of the two "accused."

Evidence suggested that the two students were prevented from coming to class on time, because a student from another class detained them in the rest-room. The defense lawyer pleaded an excellent case, but the DA convincingly stated, "Tardy is tardy." The judge imposed as punishment to copy the Constitution three times. An appeal reduced the sentence. The students need copy only Article III, the material being studied at that time in class.

During the school year, every student presented a project on a controversial issue, such as prayers in public schools, abortion, a balanced budget, the electoral college, the death penalty, the Iran/Iraq War, etc. A lively discussion followed each presentation.

Last year's presidential primaries were an added incentive to learn more about elections and the presidency. Students polled their parents and other adults, tabulating the results. The students then voted with a secret ballot, later defending their choices.

A study of state and local government involved visits from local officials. A police officer demonstrated an arrest, using a student "victim."

Project Business was an experience in economics. A businessman visited the class once a week during the second semester. Students received play money whenever they did something special. In a study of the stock market, students used play money to buy stocks. One day, the businessman asked how

Mr. Pribram with students at the Union Junior High School (National Junior Honor Society)

many students had made money on the stock market that week. Eight students raised their hands. The businessman then became the "government", requiring them to pay him taxes!

Students learned the power of advertising, developing their own singing commercials for candy.

An auction, in which students used their play money to bid for posters, T-shirts, mugs, and even a leather jacket, concluded the course. Money raised during the year was used for a pizza party, at which their businessman advisor was guest of honor.

The textbook was not neglected, and tests and homework had their place, but the real learning came, or was at least reinforced, through the firsthand contacts and hands-on experience the students enjoyed!

Some students' evaluation of this civics course includes the following: "I really enjoyed learning about government and how I can affect it." It was a fun course; we had a lot of class discussion," and "It did not just ask us a bunch of facts, but taught us to understand the principles of government.

The 1990 civics course was even more exciting. The generation is filled with high hopes and high expectations for the future.

When President Bush gave his speech on "Drugs," the students listened with great interest and responded by writing a letter to the President. They committed themselves to a drug-free class and to help those in need of help. They were thrilled to receive an answer from the President: "By recognizing the dangers of illegal drugs, and by taking steps to inform others, you have become an important part of the effort to achieve a drug-free America. His letter continued: "I am heartened by your commitment. You will set a positive example for those around you by remaining drug-free." *

When the class was comparing democracy with dictatorship a TV channel tapped segments of our class activities and the students could see themselves on the evening news!

In November and December 1989 I was glued to our TV set. The most unbelievable thing was happening. The Berlin Wall came down! And in Prague, on the same square, where in 1938 I had experienced the end of democracy in Czechoslovakia, young people started a peaceful revolution that made Czechoslovakia a free country again. This was something I never really expected to happen during my lifetime.

My students knew about my personal experiences escaping from Czechoslovakia; they were extremely interested in the breathtaking events in

*See Appendix 'Letter from President Bush' and An Unusually Exciting Civics Course

Eastern Europe. They were very much impressed by the courageous leadership of Vaclav Havel, the newly elected President, who had just come out of prison a few months earlier, and the amazing leadership he provided for his nation.

Our U.S. Senator Jim Inhofe spent a whole hour with the students answering questions about our government and the issues we face in the world.

A state senator talked to the students at a time when a most innovative education reform bill was being debated in the Oklahoma Legislature. The students did not have school for one week while teachers went on strike, successfully pressuring the Legislature to implement the much-needed reforms. The city of Tulsa was changing from a Commissioner type city government to a mayor-council city government. Many students had the opportunity to listen to the newly elected mayor of Tulsa, Rodger Randle, who was guest speaker at the National Junior Honor Society Induction ceremony at our school.

Earth Day and city problems about the environment inspired the students to write a letter to the mayor. Again they were thrilled to get a thoughtful reply.

They discovered that a citizen whether old or young could be heard and can make a difference!

In a recent letter to the "Tulsa World", I expressed my views on the *privilege of teaching:*

. . . An educator who believes in academic excellence fights an almost losing battle. Somehow we have developed a strange value system.

Even though basketball, football, golf and other sports are important, it seems they are considered more important than academic excellence . . . The extra time and effort put forth by a coach outside of regular school hours are rewarded with extra salary. The endless hours spent in preparation of classes and science labs, or on the grading of papers done by teachers in the departments of English, Social Studies, Sciences and Math, and the time they spend helping individual students go unnoticed and unrewarded.

A teacher who is entrusted with the education of the coming generation is sometimes considered a second class citizen with little support from parents of students, or even administrators.

. . . The dedicated teachers will continue to follow their calling regardless of the strange value system that fails to give top priority to academic excellence and real education.

Real education is to impart the joyful discovery of knowledge, the art to use it to improve human relations and thus create a better world. According to Webster, 'Education of a people is measured by its ideals and principles.'

John G. Pribram with students
at Union Junior High School

John G. Pribram, president
Mandy Mahan, and secre-
tary Tracey DeDominick of
the National Junior Honor
Society. Union Junior High
School, April 1989.

John Pribram at his desk, Union Jr. High School, April 1989

John's dog Bucky, April 1999

CHAPTER 14
First Visit in Fifty-Four Years To Prague, Czechoslovakia

In May 1992 I retired from teaching at Union Junior High School. This enabled my wife and me to visit my hometown in Prague, for the first time since 1938, in the fall of 1992. My wife Agnete had never been to the "Golden City". It was a unique experience for both of us.

When in Prague, we discovered to our great delight, that my eighty three year old cousin was still alive.

We spent a memorable afternoon in her small apartment. Our family home, where my cousin lived as a child, was confiscated by the Gestapo, and later the Communists took it over to provide a home for Chinese diplomats. My cousin gave us a painting of Prague, done by herself, let us choose one of the cushions she had embroidered and finally produced a golden medal with the picture of our grandfather that she wanted me to have.

She served us German "Lebkuchen", that she had saved for a special occa-

Family Villa
Confiscated by the Germans
and by the Communists

sion and then put us to shame by asking: "Do you need any money? Can I give you some?" This lady had survived both National Socialism and Communism. In spite of all her suffering, she was free from prejudice, bitterness and hatred. She was a most gracious lady.

It was quite an experience to be on Wenceslas Square, where I had stood, when the 1938 Munich agreement was announced. This deprived Czechoslovakia of the Sudetenland and later led to the Nazi take-over. It was on the same square, that the "Velvet" Revolution freed Czechoslovakia from Communism in 1989. One of my classmates from the 1937-38 school days welcomed us and took us on a tour of the city in his car. We visited the place where the Nazi SS leader Heydrich was killed by the Czechs. As a result of that action, Hitler ordered the destruction of an entire village, Lidice, near Prague.

We visited my family home, my old school and the Prague castle. We were shown the place, where Jan Masaryk, foreign minister of Czechoslovakia 1945-48, was thrown out of the window just prior to the 1948 take over by the Communists. (In 1948 I had visited Jan Masaryk at the United Nations in New York, just before he returned to Prague.)

Thousands of tourists from all around the world are visiting the "Golden City", yet the population is polite, friendly and hospitable. When I wondered about this unusual outgoing friendliness by everyone we met, I was told: "For forty-one years Prague was like a prison; now the gates are wide open and we are free. We want to link up with the whole world and be respected again. The Communists tried to kill our souls and make robots out of us, but they did not succeed."

Everywhere in Prague private enterprise is flourishing and old sites are being painted and renovated. I also went to an old six-story apartment house where President Havel lives. He was out of town, but I gave his secretary a copy of *Horizons of Hope*, in which I pay tribute to President Havel.

Three years ago such an atmosphere of communication, joy and hope would have been unheard of, but after the "Velvet" Revolution and President Havel's success in getting all Russian soldiers to leave the country, things are different.

In fact, most recently a treaty of friendship between Czechoslovakia and Germany was ratified by both Parliaments. President Havel had previously apologized for the cruelties committed by my countrymen, expelling 2.5 million Sudeten Germans immediately after World War II. The German Federal President Von Weizsäcker in turn had apologized for the Nazi occupation of Czechoslovakia. This historic reconciliation gives us hope for a brighter future.

(In January 1993 Czecho-slovakia divided into the Czech Republic and Slovakia. It was a peaceful divorce. Havel was elected President of the Czech Republic. Both countries are democracies.)

After the breathtaking events that happened in Eastern Europe in the fall of 1989, it is only appropriate to pay tribute to Vaclav Havel, then newly elected president of Czechoslovakia, by giving excepts of his speech to the U.S. Congress on February 21, 1990:

"When they arrested me on October 27, I was living in a country ruled by the most conservative Communist government of Europe, and our society slumbered beneath the pall of a totalitarian system.

"Today less than four months later, I am speaking to you as a representative of a country that has set out on the road to democracy. A country where there is complete freedom of speech, which is getting ready for free elections, and which wants to create a prosperous market and its own foreign policy. It is all very extraordinary.

"We still don't know how to put morality ahead of politics, science and economy. We are still incapable of understanding that the only genuine backbone of all our actions, if they are to be moral, is responsibility - responsibility to something higher than my family, my country, my success.

"If I subordinate my political behavior to this imperative, mediated to me by my conscience, I can't go far wrong. If on the contrary, I were not guided by this voice, not even ten presidential schools with 2,000 of the best political scientists in the world could help me. This is why I ultimately decided after resisting for a long time, to accept the burden of political responsibility.

"When Thomas Jefferson wrote that governments are instituted among men deriving their just powers from the consent of the governed, it was simple and important act of the human spirit. What gave meaning to that act, however, was the fact that the author backed it up with his life. It was not just his words: it was his deeds as well."

CHAPTER 14
The Joys of Retirement

After our most inspiring visit to my native country, Agnete and I participated in the creation of a group of Tulsa Friends of Czechs and Slovaks. I did not realize what an interesting and rewarding time retirement would be.

That group now has close to one hundred members. With receptions for the Czech ambassador to Washington, dinners for special groups coming from

Agnete at Kid's World

the Czech or Slovak Republic, participation in "Kids' World," and above all a most enjoyable Christmas party with Czech and Slovak food, we keep alive the memories and traditions of our native country and keep up to date as to what is happening over there.

One day, the Tulsa city auditor phoned me with an invitation to meet six mayors who were arriving from the Czech Republic to study city governments in the United States. Of course I accepted, and when I met the visitors I had the pleasure of finding out that one mayor came from the city of Pribram. He was as surprised as I and could not believe that he would ever meet a Pribram in Oklahoma. He was overjoyed and made me "honorary citizen of the city of Pribram" That meant very much to me.

Once retired, we had many opportunities to visit our extended families, my older brother and family in Washington, D.C. and Agnete's brother and sisters in Denmark. Those were most enjoyable and meaningful times.

John's brother Otto (center), cousin Karl, Otto's children Jeff and Jan, grandchildren Krissie and Jay Jay.

Agnete with brother and sisters Eva, Kirsten, Lars, Didi and Agnete.

Horizons of Hope was published just before I retired, and the principal and the staff of the junior high school had a great book signing party for me.

For several days afterwards, loudspeakers in the school urged all the students to buy the book. The newspaper and TV carried reviews, and as a result I had several invitations to speak to the Rotary, Lions and other civic clubs. I also spoke at many church organizations, starting with the Methodist Men and Women at the Tulsa Asbury United Methodist Church where Agnete and I have been members. I also enjoyed talking to students in various schools about World War II.

Just after the publication of *Horizons of Hope* I received a phone call from my nephew, who asked how many books he might buy for fifty dollars? It showed me more than anything else how important it is for us "seniors" to write about our own experiences, even if it's just for one's own family!

Agnete and me with Horizons of Hope.

Book signing
Principal Larry Elliott, myself,
language teacher, Becky Jack.

Agnete's father, Professor Erik Husfeldt, had signed the United Nations Charter for Denmark in San Francisco in 1945. Thus it was very natural that we join the United Nations Association of Eastern Oklahoma. We soon became very involved as officers and board members, and some time later as president of the association, I was responsible for the United Nations dinner given at the Tulsa Country Club. We always invited interesting guest speakers, some of whom were ambassadors to the United Nations. Another important activity was to support the Model United Nations Program for students.

It was an honor, then, to be invited to join the Military Order of the Purple Heart, and that led to an annual essay competition for high school students on what it means to be an American. The generous help of several banks made it possible for us to offer $2,000, $1,500, and $1,000 U.S. Savings bonds as prizes, and that, in turn, led several hundred Tulsa high school students to write essays on topics such as "Old Glory," "The Ballot Box," and "Freedom Is Not Free."

Veteran's Day Parade

The essays showed that this new generation of Americans is patriotic and optimistic about the future. Most of the participants wrote outstanding essays so it was difficult to choose from among so many excellent essays. The local TV frequently came to our awards assemblies and aired excerpts of the winning essays on Memorial Day. We also participated in the annual Veterans' Day parade on November 11.

John Pribram presenting the Military Order of the Purple Heart Leadership Award to J.R.O.T.C. Tulsa high school students.

It is very moving to experience the gratitude expressed by the public for veterans.

I was also asked to work on a committee sponsored by the Friends of the Tulsa Public Library devoted to "Great Decisions." We have now eight groups discussing each year eight major world issues suggested by the Foreign Policy Association. This is done all across the country, and after each discussion participants fill out ballots that are sent to the Foreign Policy Association, which tabulates them and sends the results to the State Department, to congress, and to the White House. It is a way for the average citizen to influence our foreign policy and for those of us participating to keep up with what is happening in the world.

I also had many rewarding experiences as mediator for "Early Settlement," a part of the Tulsa City Court system. At first one has to be trained and then certified by the State Supreme Court. Our task is to help opposing parties-neighbors against neighbors, merchants against consumers, landlords against tenants, realtors and others-to find a solution to their problems by just talking about their concerns with one another in a confidential, voluntary, out-of-court proceeding.

In the springtime another rewarding experience is to volunteer to help others prepare their tax returns. One day a lady was so excited getting a refund she got up and kissed me. The next man waiting to get help with his forms approached me and simply said, "I promise you, I am not going to kiss you!"

I also joined the Tulsa Committee on Foreign Relations. Every month at a very special dinner meeting we listen to interesting speakers dealing with foreign policy.

"One day I got a phone call from Germany from the son of one of my Berlin friends. He asked, whether he could come to Tulsa for a week, because he was making a documentary about his father's life. His father had told him, that my life had profoundly changed him. He wanted to discover for himself my part in his father's life.

A Berlin Educator, his father, was a Nazi during WWII and participated in German occupation of my home in Prague, Czechoslovakia.

After the war he attended a conference for the Moral Re-Armanment of Nations in Caux Switzerland. There I spoke to the 800 delegates and I apologized for the hatred I had had against the Germans. A large group of Germans were there for the very first time.

His father just couldn't take it and wanted to leave. A Danish friend suggested that at least he should to talk to me. We got together—the former enemies became friends—and his outlook on life changed completely.

From then on till now, he has visited the Czech Republic many times, building bridges between the Germans and the Czechs.

His son and a photographer spent a whole week in Tulsa, following everything I was doing and meeting some of my friends, in fact even our home was changed into a film studio.

He wanted to go to church with us and was permitted to film everything, except the time during the sermon. He concluded that the minister had been talking about the same things, we had been discussing all week long!

When he left, he wrote in our guest book: "Learning from the past, we hope to gain much for the future."

CHAPTER 15
Agnete's Going "Home"

The teacher's salary is rather small, but Agnete managed it very well. She loved her family, her Danish friends, and her country, so we kept saving enough to be able to visit them and her friends in Denmark about every three years.

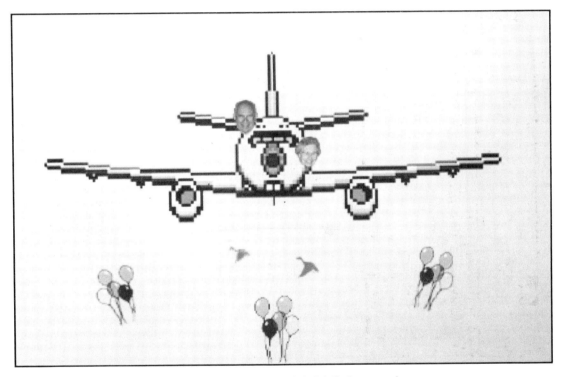

Invitation to the Danish birthday party

Finally a few years ago, I inherited some money from a family home in the Czech Republic. Now we could do something that Agnete had wanted to do for a long time. In Denmark the practice is that the "birthday child" gives the party. Agnete was going to be seventy.

This was the time to invite all the family (thirty-five of them) to the birthplace of her ancestors and have a wonderful party in a special restaurant she had picked the year before. At that time she also celebrated with others their 50-year high school reunion.

Agnete and her brother Lars

Agnete had worked on this for a whole year. She had spent hours on the computer creating the invitation. She had been in touch right through the year with the restaurants about the menu she had ordered. She had prepared place cards and worked on the seating arrangement, making sure that everybody would have the best time. And of course she thought very carefully about the talk she should make as the honored birthday child. Her brother Lars was the master of ceremonies, and his wife, Helle, had written a very special song about Agnete. Other family members helped to make this a wonderful celebration. It was a very moving time. I can say now God had prepared it to make this the most memorable experience for all.

Agnete also found another nice place where we could invite some of our Danish friends for a party (twenty-five came). It was a very rich experience for all that came.

And then one day our world of joyful retirement was suddenly turned upside down.

The hardest and saddest moment of my life happened when two policemen and a police chaplain came to tell me that Agnete had been killed by a 92-year-old driver. It was shock of all shocks. However, I knew one thing: that one had to accept what had happened and turn to God for help.

I began to do things which had to be done, automatically, almost in a daze—telephone calls of course to my Washington family, to Agnete's family and friends in Denmark and to my closest friends in Tulsa.

Many friends began coming in to help, especially Reverend Bill Mason, who suggested the funeral home. I asked him to do the Memorial Service as well as the interment ceremony at the cemetery. The Reverend Norman Bolin came with his wife Linda and I asked him to do the Eulogy and Linda to do the Lord's Prayer in sign language. Both Buddy and Reverend Mason came back the next day to talk about the service and what they might say. (No one who knew Agnete will be surprised that all these details had been prepared in anticipation of the day when one of us would go home.)

Fortunately, Bob Marks, a friend from the Military Order of the Purple Heart took me by hand to visit the funeral home where I had to select an appropriate casket. I chose one with birds flying into the sky. It was very beautiful.

 Bob then took me to the cemetery, yet another new experience. (A few years earlier, Agnete had insisted that we buy a burial plot.) I had to make all kinds of decisions there as well. Finally Bob invited me to lunch, saying simply, "You need one hot meal a day." Back at home suddenly a lady appeared whom I hardly knew: the new president of the Friends of the Tulsa Public Library. She offered to help anyway she could. She took care of the phone calls, while I was away from the home. I was most grateful. She also read my book while there. Amazing!

I knew I had to turn to God for everything. I was no longer able to ask Agnete for her guidance. This was a new basic turning point in my life. From now on, He would be the only one to help me. He gives me guidance from the moment I wake up each morning, just as I had done when I first learned how to walk. I wrote down all the thoughts that came to me. I measured them by the four absolute moral standards of honesty, purity, unselfishness, and love. Most of the time I knew very clearly what God wanted me to do. Many times in the past I had discovered that true **JOY** comes when one puts **Jesus** first, then **Others**, and only then **Yourself**.

During those difficult days, there was no time to think about myself. I had to plan for the guests coming from Tucson, three nurses from St. Louis, and for my brother and his family on the day of the memorial service. Again, it was not I, but God working through me.

The Tulsa World covered the funeral on its front page to reach the entire community:

TULSA WORLD

Victim remembered for her spirit, love of people

February 25, 2000

By NICHOLE MARSHALL
World Staff Writer

Agnete Pribram

She lived through the German Occupation of Denmark during World War II.

Agnete Pribram was killed Wednesday when a driver crashed into a drugstore. Befitting a woman who spent her life working to make the world a better place, mourners from across the globe are grieving Agnete Pribram's death.

Pribram, 70, was killed Wednesday when she was struck by a car as she walked into the Med-X Drugstore at 3133 S. Harvard Ave. A 92-year-old woman said her foot slipped off her brake pedal onto the accelerator causing her Buick to jump a curb and crash into the store front.

The article went on to describe how persons from across the world were phoning to offer their condolences and their support. I told them how I recalled last seeing Agnete before she left to meet some friends for lunch Wednesday. She looked exceptionally beautiful, dressed in black with a brightly colored scarf, and the last thing I said to her was, "You really look good." Friends later told me that she had a wonderful, lively, and exciting luncheon with her friends. Then, shortly after three p.m., the police came to our front door to bring the bad news. They also brought the scarf she had been wearing in the car. The newspaper article continued with some background information:

"Agnete Pribram was born in Copenhagen, Denmark, and lived through the German occupation of her country during World War II. She remained a Danish citizen. Her father was one of the leaders of the Danish resistance during World War II and was one of the persons who signed the charter for the United Nations in 1945 . . . Her father and her family helped to save many Jews.

Agnete Pribram graduated as a registered nurse from FA Hillerød in Denmark. As she started nursing she also discovered there is much more she was meant to do... For many years, she worked as a full-time volunteer with Moral Re-Armament, which worked toward the reconstruction of democracy and reconciliation in Europe after World War II. She later worked with the international musical touring group *Up With People*. She was one of the first ones in that group, a group of people who believe there is something good in every one of us; all they need is to find it. While traveling with *Up With People*, she met John Pribram, who was born in what is now the Czech Republic and was working as an educator with the group.

The couple married in 1968 and settled in Tulsa in 1971. Agnete then worked for the University of Michigan's Institute for Social Research, the nation's longest-standing laboratory for interdisciplinary research in the social sciences. Pribram said he is still in shock about the tragic death of his beloved wife. "There is no blame about what happened . . . Unfortunately . . . things like this do happen. She was a caring person who, in everyone she met, saw a royal soul who should be supported and encouraged regardless of what happened . . . She had a sense of humor. She really loved people. She loved nature. She loved music, and she enjoyed traveling. It was a privilege to be married to her. She was an amazing lady. Agnete Pribram is survived by her husband and three sisters, a brother and their families, who live in Denmark. The couple was in Denmark in the fall, when they celebrated Agnete's seventieth birthday with a party that she had spent several years organizing.

I thought its amazing that she could still do all that. Her friends and her family in Denmark remember her from that party, with fond memories. In some ways, that experience for her was a real highlight in her life. Who knows? Maybe it was time. Maybe she was meant to go home now and it was her time."

Jarvis Harriman, a good friend of mine describes best the "Memorial Service", taken from the book *In Memory of Agnete:*

Agnete's Memorial Service

Family and close friends of Agnete Husfeldt Pribram gathered in the Rose Hill Cemetery in Tulsa, Oklahoma on Monday, February 28 to pay their respects in a service of burial. It was a lovely, balmy and sunny afternoon at the gravesite. Her husband John was supported by his elder brother Otto and Otto's son Jeff and daughter Jan Gutierrez and Jeff's wife Ditas, who had flown that morning from Washington, D.C.

The casket was crowned by a bright array of roses, carnations and chrysanthemums in pink, white and yellow. At Agnete's feet was a traditional Cherokee Indian blanket in blue with red and yellow accents, the high honor of this Native American people expressing love and warmth. It was presented

to John by a member of the Cherokee Nation at the conclusion of the grave-side service.

Flowers and messages from Agnete's brother and three sisters, with nieces and nephews from Denmark were at the Pribram home and surrounded the altar in the Asbury Methodist Church for the memorial service that followed the interment.

Fellow members of Agnete's nursing profession from her years with Moral Re-Armament and *Up With People* joined the family, traveling from Grand Rapids, Michigan, St. Louis, Missouri and Tucson, Arizona.

The city's principal newspaper, the Tulsa World, had roused the population to the tragic accident in which Agnete died on Wednesday, February 23, with two front-page stories and Agnete's photograph.

An outpouring of sympathy for John was matched by tributes of love, gratitude and affection from countless citizens, and from members of the many organizations Agnete and John have worked with since they moved to Tulsa in 1971.

At the church, the gathering sang a hymn Agnete had herself selected, J.S. Bach's "Jesus Joy of Our Desiring." The church's music minister sang Jerusalem the "Holy City," and accompanying himself on the guitar, "Edelweiss." A family friend, the Reverend Bill Mason, led the prayers at the cemetery and at the church. The Reverend Norman Bolin, Jr., gave the eulogy. He had married a young Cherokee woman who had been a high school student of John's in the *Up With People* traveling high school in 1970. He told the audience of how Agnete and John had grilled him about his intentions as he had been courting Linda Leaf. It was she who had presented the Cherokee blanket. She performed the Lord's Prayer in the American Indian Sign Language to accompany the music minister who sang the Prayer.

This was truly a celebration of Agnete's life. Several hundred people joined the Pribram family for a reception at the church after the service. Members of Agnete's Beta Sigma Phi Sorority, the Military Order of the Purple Heart, and other groups with whom Agnete and John have participated. Refreshments were provided by the Tulsa Friends of Czechs and Slovaks. John's brother e-mailed the next day: "We were all very much impressed and moved by the wonderful service and caring and love your friends expressed."

A close friend had told John that this might well be the hardest day of his life. Instead John found it to be one of the most enriching and inspiring days of his life, and he wished that all those who sent messages or flowers could have experienced it personally with him.

—Jarvis Harriman

It was indeed a sad day, but I was grateful that there were people who cared and who came to the magnificent funeral service. My brother, his two children, and many other friends helped me then in many ways, and in that sense it was a very rich time.

When all was done, my guidance came. Somehow God again helped me to find a new purpose in life, to pass on the wonderful things He had given us throughout the years. I would write a book *In Memory of Agnete.*

John with Every Day Hero Award

I had cancelled a flight Agnete and I had previously booked to attend the thirty-fifth reunion of *Up With People* in Florida. We had both wanted to go, but now Agnete was no more in this world. Then again, guidance came: "You have to go. Agnete would want you to go." Not only that, guidance came to pay the conference fee for twenty former *Up With People* students, who otherwise would not have been able to attend. I am sure Agnete would have also enjoyed doing that! Now I had to go there alone. But it was a privilege meeting many of my former students and accepting a special "Every Day Hero" award for Agnete and myself. If anyone really deserved it, it was my beloved wife.

Knud Simon Christiansen described the Orlando Reunion in the book "In Memory of Agnete:"

Agnete would have loved to have been there at the greatest ever gathering some 2,000 alumni and family members of alumni when *Up With People* celebrated its thirty-fifth alumni reunion in Orlando, Florida. Agnete and John had, in fact, already reserved their passages to Orlando when the fatal accident happened. Agnete would have loved to be just there. Humanly speaking, she ought to have been there at the Orlando 2000 thirty-fifth *Up With People* alumni reunion where, posthumously, she was bestowed with the James MacLennan "Everyday Hero" award.

Altogether seven chosen "Everyday Heroes" were honored for what they have accomplished through their every day life. Two of them were Agnete and John. The event took place at the President's brunch that highlighted the reunion bringing together so many repre-senatives of the 18,000 alumni who have participated in more than a hundred casts of *Up With People*. John was introduced by Forrest "Duffy" Bledsoe, co-founder and a past president of the *Up With People* International Alumni Association, who told the audience how

Agnete and John had changed his life and helped him to find a firm belief in God.

He also mentioned Agnete and John's deep involvement in American society in Tulsa, Oklahoma after their time on the road. No doubt they were "everyday heroes." As John was being introduced, alumni from the *Up With People* High School, who knew Agnete and John from those first years of *Up With People* rushed to the podium to stand by John and endorse with their presence what "Duffy" gave in words on their behalf.

John told about his background for joining *Up With People*, how he had lost his country, his parents, and his leg as a combat medic in the U.S. Army in eastern France. In the hospital he met Blanton Belk's sisters who helped him let God take care of his bitterness and hatred toward the Germans. He met and married the Danish nurse Agnete Husfeldt who, having lived through five years under German occupation, had experiences similar to John's. For five years they were on the staff of *Up With People* in Germany and in America helping create the Up With People High School.

John closed by saying that in accepting this special award he would like to emphasize that for the last thirty-two years it was Agnete who had kept him on this good road. She really was an everyday hero! Numerous were the people who, after the bestowal of the award, came to John and testified to the difference Agnete and John had made in their lives. Agnete would have loved to be present, not so much because of the award but because of these people who have carried the spirit of *Up With People* to so many corners of the Earth. In memory of Agnete, John had invited twenty alumni from Agnete's casts to the reunion in Orlando. "This is what Agnete would want me to do," said John.

Many participants in the reunion bought the book *Horizons of Hope* in which John tells his own story and that of his meeting with Agnete. The proceeds of the sale he gave to Global Teen Challenge, a forum in the framework of the reunion where teens aged 13 to 19 sparked an interactive dialogue about issues effecting teens everywhere, especially in their own communities. Their aim: To inform, engage and motivate young people to serve their communities. Their strategy: To strengthen the voice of youth through *Up With People.*

Those former *UWP* students invited John for a special luncheon, where they gave him a huge letter signed by each one of them expressing how much he and Agnete had meant to them.

One alumnus from a later year (Cast 75C) after the luncheon put the following on the letter: "Your lives, your devotion to your wife and students made the award you received a true example of what a true everyday hero is. This was a pure moment and that melted this cynic's heart. I cannot express fully in words what I felt but suffice to say you made me believe in true goodness again." Agnete would have loved that! She was there in spirit. One of them simply said, "She is smiling at us."

Now I was alone, experiencing God's wonderful guidance in a new way. What a new situation for someone, who had learned so much from his inspired wife. Yet the house needed cleaning. Again, a friend suggested a cleaning lady. One problem solved. What to do with Agnete's clothing? Again there was a friend in charge of a store that sells goods and uses the money for needy children. She came and took it all. All the photo equipment? The camera store Agnete worked with took it on consignment. I had never been there and as I turned over the equipment, I just cried. How about the lighting

John receiving the "Everyday Hero Award". supported by his former UWP students: Charmaine, Jaine, Vici, Don Lyberger, Sally W., Pat Berry, John R., Jeff Petersen, Gloria Collins, Tom Kieffer.

equipment that filled one of our rooms? A student at the camera store heard about it. He wanted to build his own studio, so he came, and for a small price, he bought it all. What about the car? Our neighbor bought it. He wanted to go to Pennsylvania. His car was much older, so he bought Agnete's.

Agnete always felt our garage door needed to be replaced. Very quickly I got in touch with a firm. Just before they were going to install the new door, the old one broke. Termites were discovered and a carpenter needed to do the job. Again came divine intervention, at first it seemed impossible that the carpenter, an over busy man, could do the job. Yet he came the same evening to fix it all.

The insurance company called. One agent visited me. He got so interested in my experiences that he bought a copy of *Horizons of Hope*. "Do not deal with the Insurance company yourself," my friends told me. Again a lawyer, the son of one of Agnete's best friend who had died of cancer, took it on and dealt with it.

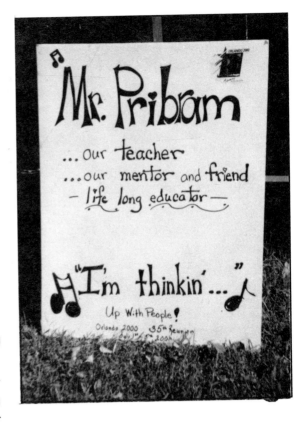

Phone calls coming in. Money given to the church in Agnete's memory, to the United Nations Association of Eastern Oklahoma, to the Friends of the Public Library, to the Indian Health Center, a rose being planted in her memory at the Tulsa Rose Garden. Some may call it coincidence. I call it "God's wonderful guidance." Of course life it is at times very difficult. In church, when I realized that from now on I would go without Agnete, I just cried. At the cemetery I cried, and the hundreds of letters coming in, make me cry.

I never knew I was so emotional, but I'm told crying is healthy. With God's help and Jesus as my best friend, the future is going to be the best ever! I was able to send a booklet in Agnete's memory as a thank you gift to the hundreds of friends, who supported me in those difficult, but very rich days.

The only thing I could do to deal with this new and very painful situation was to go straight back to God. Years ago in my quiet time, He promised to give me Agnete as my wife. She had been my very best friend for thirty-two years and special occasions.

Now we discovered that the Nordic Heritage Museum in Seattle, Washington, had National costumes from every Scandinavian country, except Denmark.

I decided to give this cos-tume along with the book *In Memory of Agnete* to the museum. This is a real and last-ing tribute to Agnete and to Denmark.

From Agnete's youngest sister I received a most meaningful gift. Her late husband, another resistance leader, had a neck tie which only resistance leaders wear at special occasions.

She wanted to give this tie to me. Again I cried, grateful for all the care from Agnete's family. The only thing I could do to deal with this new and very painful situation was to go straight back to God.

Years ago in my quiet time, He prom-ised to give me Agnete as my wife. She had been my very best friend for thirty-two years and has helped and inspired me in everthing I have been doing. Now He took her home and she is with Jesus, smiling at me and all of us here on earth.

CHAPTER 16
Without Agnete

Six years ago Agnete left us to join Jesus. Since that event she has been smiling at me and all of us as we continue our journey here.

For me those six years were, at first, very difficult. Agnete had spoiled me, and done every thing for me—helped me to enjoy life to the fullest. Now I had to go to the grocery store, had to fix my own meals, to make the bed, to clean the house and all those other tasks she had done and I had never done.

I was all alone, except for "Bucky" our dog. Agnete loved Bucky. Looked after him, played with and considered him her special friend. Bucky and I missed her terribly – but time helped the two of us to accept her absence.

The following letter is from Bucky to a friend . . .

Bucky Pribram
13 yr. old Sheltie Mix
May 1, 2005

Dear Melville:

I was thrilled when, last night, speaking from Scotland to my master here in Tulsa, you inquired about me. You are what I call a *friend*. Let me answer your inquiry:

Sometimes John keeps reading the newspaper, or even falls asleep in his chair. When I finally am able to awaken him we take one of our daily two walks a day.

A walk is an adventure for me. I look for anything I can find. One day I even found a dead bird which did not thrill my master at all!

Recently on one of our walks I felt very sick. By evening I felt so bad I hid in a corner in the yard. After I went in the house I hid behind a chair. Clearly John became very concerned.

I did not eat for four days and even refused the medicine that John tried to give me. After two days at the vet I felt much better and returned home feeling happy and healthy.

When my master goes to PetsMart I am allowed to go with him and we shop together. I really enjoy how other customers "make" over me. And just think, I am about seventy years old!

My daily routine includes two good meals with a stick for dessert. John also brushes me twice a day, which I admit I am not crazy about, but we play and have fun when the brushing is over.

I also play tricks on John: once I took his socks into the yard and buried them. He could only find one!

John swims in our pool twice every day [in the summer!], but I do not like to get wet, so I just keep watch over him to make sure that all is ok.

Another trick I play on him is to hide his hearing-aid box. It takes him forever to find it and he even blames the housekeeper for hiding it.

One afternoon when John came home I did not greet him, but I barked. He looked all over for me but could not find me. Finally he looked in the bathroom, and there I was. I had locked myself in!

Well, Melville, I hope you see that I have a pretty good time. I look forward to you inquiring about me again.

Bucky

In the spring of 2005 after spending 13 wonderful years in our household, Bucky died of cancer. To lose Bucky was in some ways almost as difficult as losing Agnete. I lived through three difficult days and decided never to have a dog again, but kept on searching for God's plan for my life.

The morning meditation has become the most important part of my daily life.

In the fall of 2005 my heart opened to SKIPPY this is what he says . . .

February 2006

Dear Friend,

Probably you will be very surprised to hear from me. I'm Skippy, the new dog, in the Pribram household. John told me that his friends will also be my friends.

I'm still in my puppy years. I'm a rescue dog and most grateful to have been taken in to such a nice home. I have made it my own and I guard the house and the yard to the best of my ability.

John told me I'm a very good watchdog and he has never felt as secure as now.

I would like to share with you some of my recent experiences.

One stormy night with a lot of lightning and thunder, which frightened me, I clung to my master, who tried to calm me down.

One morning, when he went to get the newspaper I skipped out just to visit some neighbor dogs, John quickly found me and brought me home.

I love to play with a sock and a ball. I want my master to continue all day long and I get very upset when he wants to quit and I bark and bark to tell him to keep playing, but alas it does not seem to work.

The only thing for me to do is to run into the yard to chase squirrels – I love doing that, but I have not been able to catch them either.

I love to play tricks on John – I had carted one of his slippers into the yard, and then one of his overshoes. I like to break pencils, especially when I am bored – but I also like to lighten up my master – just think of his surprise when I jumped into the bathtub with him!

I enjoy watching my master swim in our pool, but I hate the water. Twice I accidentally fell into the pool – but I crawled out as quickly as I could.

One night. John wanted to watch the Oklahoma-Kansas football game. I wanted to play, jump on him and grab his hands – he disliked it and almost got mad at me. I curled up and accidentally detached the electrical cord-imagine no football!

We do go to obedience school. I like it. I learned how to sit still, especially when I get a reward, I learned how to stand still and now I'm learning how to heal, which is really fun!

When we go on walks we usually stay together, but one time he wanted to go one way and I wanted to another way – I slipped out of my collar with its identification. John was very frightened. He said, "a dog without a tag may very well be picked up and put to sleep!" I let him look for me for a time, but then I came back. That very day a new and stronger collar was put on me.

On a grocery store trip there was a poor lonely dog watching us. Both of us wondered what he was doing, then I just accidentally opened the car door window and jumped out joining the dog –the master stopped the car and looked for us. Fortunately, he found us nearby and I was once more reunited with him.

Every day is different. Every day is full of surprises. We are a great team together. We care for each other and I'm most grateful to become a friend of his friends!

One day, moving from the kitchen to the dining room, my master slipped and fell. He had terrible pains and could not walk. Fortunately, Buddy Bolin, the minister who delivered the Eulogy for Agnete at her Memorial Service, came to his rescue – a trip to the emergency room at St. John's Hospital revealed a small break in his hip. In a quick operation, four screws were inserted.

He spent three and a half weeks in the hospital. I was lonely, staying home alone, but I had a job to do – to protect our home.

Our neighbor came every day to walk and feed me and others came to play with me.

When John finally came home again, I gave him an overwhelming welcome. John and I are no longer "master and dog, we are "dear friends."

Of course I love to "skip out" if only to the yard.

After all, I am Skippy

Get Well Wishes

Those weeks in the hospital were absolutely amazing. Normally I would have spent Christmas in Washington with my brother and his family, now I was to celebrate with Skippy at home, but my brother called me at the hospital every second day.

Buddy Bolin is the minister of the United Methodist Church of the Shepherd. I had joined his church. Buddy and his wife Linda, visited me just about every day.

After two days of pain, I was free from pain, just letting my bones heal again, I asked God why this had happened.

"To have time with your friends, time for you, in this busy life, may not have otherwise".

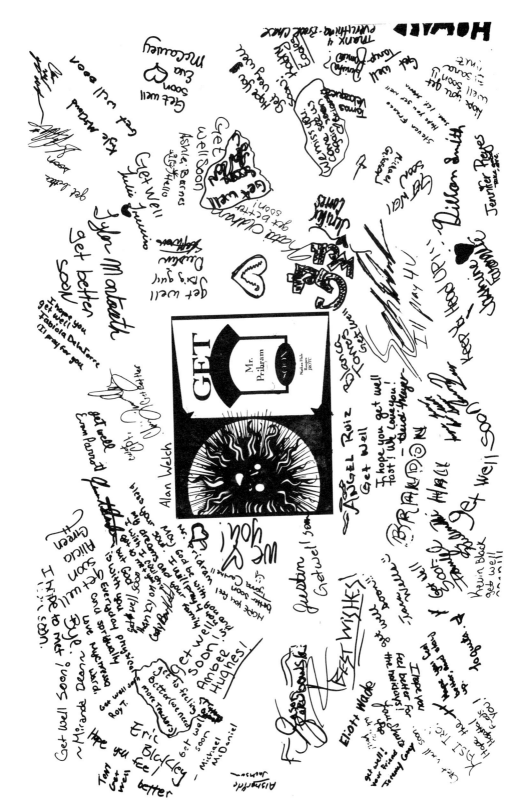

How true – over 30 friends from various organizations where I had been a member visited me. Some brought flowers and some brought gifts. I received get well wishes from many former students. (For a teacher to hear from a student, he taught over thirty years ago is an unforgettable treat).

Bob Lieser, the president of the board of the friends of the Tulsa City County Library brought me the latest book "Franklin and Winston" by Jon Meacham (an intimate portrait of an epic friendship between Roosevelt and Churchill) and Dr. Randle, professor at OU/Tulsa sent me three interesting books.

Dr. Donaldson, a director of the Tulsa Committee on Foreign relations transmitted a resolution from the committee: "Thanking you for your loyal support and wishing for your speedy return to our ranks.

"Through your faithful service to the Great Decisions program, you have helped us to recruit many fine members. We appreciate your constant presence, your good cheer, and your devotion to the cause of bringing good international programs to Tulsa".

I could give "Horizons of Hope" as a thank you to my physicians, and "In Memory of Agnete" as a thank you to the nurses. I enjoyed the hospital so much, I didn't even want to leave!

I recalled the amazing time at McGuire General Hospital, 60 years ago. That is when I learned how to walk again (See page 33).

The open heart surgery I had a few years ago, when I received a "pig valve" came to my mind. The highlight was that Agnete was there when I recovered from surgery–

And this time she was with me again. Again, looking at me from above – smiling!"

A Trip To Florida

During the summer of 2005 I decided to visit my two friends in Fort Myers – they had been among the four girls that visited me at the McGuire General Hospital and had helped me to find my way on the 'Good Road'.

I was at McGuire General Hospital as a disabled veteran.

They found me on VJ day – when every one was happy, celebrating and enjoying the end of the war –there they found me in a corner of the hospital "crying". I was lonely, discouraged, bitter with no hope for the future, even though we had just defeated our enemies.

I had not seen them for sixty years. Now I could go there and simply say

"THANK YOU" for all the help they had been to me.

We had fun exchanging our experiences. We had a great time.

In fact, they had arranged for me to talk about "Horizons of Hope" to the people in the retirement home, to a special men's breakfast and at an evening party given in my honor (See page 34-35).

Up With People (Revisited)

I went to Tucson for the second trip during the summer of 2005. It was the occasion of the 40th Anniversary of *Up With People.*

The cast that had created the first sing out in 1965 decided to put on the show they did 40 years ago and now, 40 years older. It was a fantastic experience.

This show may have been even better than the very first one – all those young men and women had become mature well rounded citizens.

I had the privilege to talk with some of my former students there, hearing over and over again how much Agnete and I had helped them during those critical teenage years traveling on the road with *Up With People.* It was a very rewarding experience.

This group of alumni is sticking together and searching for ways to have a creative impact on the world.

George Washington

In the newspapers I had read that students graduate from high school who do not know who **George Washington** was.

Just at the end of my morning meditation I had a most unusual thought – a picture of George Washington should be in the home rooms of social studies teachers in elementary, middle and senior high school.

When I mentioned this idea to my chapter of the Military Order of the Purple Heart – it was wholeheartedly endorsed. A committee was formed to work on the project – and we wondered why we had not thought of this before.

Great white hope
Snowflake changed the way
the world views apes.
Scene2 H-1

Happy returns
More people getting help with taxes.
Business E-1

Movin' up
With Kansas' loss, OSU moves into a tie for first
place in the Big 12 after defeating Texas Tech.
Sports B-1

John Lucas III (left)
and Jamende Curry

WWW.TULSAWORLD.COM
SUNDAY
FEBRUARY 20, 2005

TULSA WORLD

★★ FINAL HOME EDITION
$1.50

■ 100 YEARS ■

Meeting George Washington

John Pribram of Chapter 589 of the Military Order of the Purple Heart presents a portrait of George Washington to students at Mayo Demonstration School. Pribram is chairman of Project George Washington. The group's goal is to make presenations on the first U.S. president to every school district in Tulsa County.

More than a familiar face

▶ Veterans are visiting schools and telling students of George Washington's vital place in history

BY ANDREA EGER
World Staff Writer

He's more than just a face on the dollar bill.

That's what a local group of Purple Heart veterans want Tulsa schoolchildren to learn from Project George Washington.

Nine members of Chapter 589 of the Military Order of the Purple Heart set out to visit every school in Tulsa Public Schools by Washington's birthday, which is Tuesday.

They raised the funds to purchase 1,450 laminated, oval-shaped portraits of the first U.S. president for social studies classrooms across the district.

"It all started with the point that we read in the newspapers that there are kids graduating

- 130 -

from high school who don't even know who George Washington was. And to think, we may still be English if it weren't for George Washington!" said John Pribram, chairman of the project.

Pribram said his own organization, which is the only one chartered by Congress exclusively for combat-wounded veterans, wouldn't exist if Washington hadn't created the military honor as a general in the American Revolution.

Pribram and the other veterans have been invited to give presentations about Washington in classrooms and even school-wide assemblies.

What have they told students about Washington?

Not just the stuff his legend is made of. In fact, Pribram didn't even mention the wooden teeth or the cherry-tree chopping, when asked.

"He was a humble man. He didn't want to be called the King or 'Your Highness.' He said he would only be called 'Mr. President.' And he didn't ask for any money for what he was doing," Pribram said.

Oleta Whibbey, school counselor at Mayo Demonstration School, said students enjoyed Pribram's presentation at their schools' Monday morning assembly.

"The children were very attentive and it really did impress them. It made them want to learn more about our first president," Whibbey said.

Whibbey said she was struck by the thought that schools should be doing something for veterans – not the other way around.

"They just aren't given enough recognition. Like George was one of our forefathers, they were forerunners for our country. Where would we be without them?"

Pribram responded to that notion with the kind of humility he attributed to Washington. He said he'd gotten just as much from the experience as he has contributed.

"Basically, what hit me most was that everywhere they thanked us for the pictures, thanked us for coming and, in fact, thanked us for fighting in World War II," he said. "I didn't think about what I was getting, but it's very rewarding. And my friends are just as enthusiastic about having the privilege of doing this."

Pribram was awarded the Purple Heart, the Silver Star for gallantry, and the Bronze Star for heroism as a U.S. Army combat medic in World War II. He lost his leg while attempting to help two wounded men in a minefield.

For him, Project George Washington has been a brief return to the work he loved doing for 20 years as a social studies teacher at Monte Cassino School and Union Public Schools.

"I am overwhelmed by the quality of education we have. Looking at those kids, I feel we don't need to be worried about the future," he said.

Pribram's presentations may have given him a glimpse of the future, but for one Mayo Demonstration School teacher, Monday's assembly was a blast from her past.

"When he started talking, I thought, 'He sounds familiar.' And then I recognized him. He was one of my techers at Monte Cassino," said Susan Edwards, a pre-K and kindergarten teacher. "It was very good to see that he's so healthy and still active and I thought it was good for the students to meet someone who was a part of history."

Edwards said she thinks Project George Washington gave students not just a better understanding of Washington, but a real-life example of a World War II hero.

"When I was talking to Mr. Pribram afterward, a fourth-grade boy came up and said "My grandfather was in World War II.' I thought that was neat and showed some of the connection the kids made with this man," Edwards said.

The Military Order of the Purple Heart has already raised enough funds to bring Project George Washington to the Owasso and Broken Arrow districts. The group's goal is to get to every school district in Tulsa County.

Pribram said the wholesale cost of the portraits is about $2.50 each. For more information about the project, e-mail him at jpribram@cox.net.

Andrea Eger 581-8470
andrea.eger@tulsaworld.com

COMMUNITY WORLD

MIDTOWN

Happ
New '

Tulsa's Hm
plans cultu
Please go to

TULSA WORLD • **PAGE 1** • Wednesday, November 2, 2005 • www.tulsaworld.com

Picture this, by George

Purple Heart recipients continue Washington portrait project

BY SARA PLUMMER
World Staff Writer

SARA PLUMMER / Tulsa World

John Pribram (right), Robert Marks and Ted McDaris are members of the Tulsa chapter of the Military Order of the Purple Heart. The chapter started Project George Washington, with a goal of placing a picture of George Washington in every classroom in area schools.

He was the first president of the United States, he allegedly chopped down a cherry tree as a child, and he had wooden teeth.

These are the only facts many people remember about Geroge Washington.

Members of the Military Order of the Purple Heart are trying to change that by placing a picture of Washington in every school classroom.

"We read there were people who were graduating who didn't know who George

Washington was," said John Pribram, chairman of Project George Washington and a member of the Military Order of the Purple Heart.

Before the end of the 2004-05 school year, Pribram said, the group had donated 3,000 25-inch-by-18inch posters of the first president in Tulsa, Broken Arrow, Owasso, Union and Catoosa school districts.

Now, the group has raided enough money to donate 800 posters to schools in Jenks, Bixby, Berryhill, Collinsville, Sand Springs and

Sapulpa by Feb. 22, George Washington's birthday.

"We felt every student who has social studies should see a picture of George Washington," Pribram said. "In first grade, they see the picture; in middle school, they see the picture; and in high school they see it, so there's no way they won't know who George Washington is."

Steve Pittman, principal of the Union Eighth Grade Center, 6501 S. Garnett Road, said as a veteran, he appreciates what the organization is doing.

I'm proud of these guys still trying to get kids interested and to connect our students back to what we studied," Pittman said. "I think it's critical. We have such a rich heritage, and we're trying to connect students to history."

Chris Clark, principal at Hoover Elementary School, 2327 S. Darlington Ave. in Tulsa, said the posters are a great contribution.

"(George Washington's) picture belongs in the classroom with the American flag," Clark said. "It's provided an opportunity for teachers to discuss him."

Maj. Mike Maguffee, the senior instructor for Nathan Hale High School's Junior ROTC program, has known Pribram for 10 years and supports Project George Washington.

"My impression of (Pribram) is that he understands the importance of this generation knowing our country's roots and history, especially those that were developed and guided by our first president," he said.

Pribram said a reminder of the United States' history needs to be present in schools.

"Our history is a very neglected topic in our education," he said. "Unless you learn how you country was created, it is a very superficial life."

Maguffee agrees.

"Many students, in general, lack some basic historical knowledge, for which (the poster) provides a vehicle for discussion," he said. "(The order) brought a visual source into schools as a daily reminder of our country's first president."

Robert Marks, past National Americaism Officer for the Military Order of the Purple Heart, said he presented Project George Washington at the national convention in August.

Marks said chapters in cities such as Tucson, Ariz., were interested in starting the project in their schools.

The new National Americanism Officer will not know how the project has done nationally until chapter reports are filed in the spring, Marks said.

Pribram said Washington's picture used to hang in every classroom.

"George Washington's picture was in classrooms before, but for some reason, his picture was taken away. People in my generation wondered why he left," he said. "It's simply that the father of our country be displayed in our classroom. Why not honor the person who helped get the country started?"

Pittman said as teachers cleaned out their classrooms, pictures of George Washington were set aside to make way for new activities and decorations.

"Over time, it got relegated to the back of the closet," he said.

Pribram said the order has received numerous thank-you cards and notes from students, teachers and administrators about the project.

Mike Maguffee

"I was amazed by some of the letters that come after we started. We had not the slighest idea that would happen," he said. "I'm grateful (for the success).

"After Sept. 11, we were united and flags appeared in front of every house. Patriotism was rekindled. The George Washington project does the same thing."

The first Badge of Military Merit presented on May 3, 1783 at Headquarters.

At the banquet of the Oklahoma State Convention of the Military Order of the Purple Heart, Bob Marks, National Americanism Officer, on behalf of the National Commander Robert Lichtenberger, presented me with a picture of George Washington giving the first Badge of Military Merit to three of his men.

In my reply I thanked Bob, saying that this program, without an effective team of seven patriots visiting 145 schools and contributions of 42 patriots raising an excess of $8,000, would not have been possible.

At the 2005 National Convention of the Military Order of the Purple Heart, in his address, Bob Marks encouraged all chapters to follow Tulsa's lead.

In the fall of 2005 some 80,000 students in Tulsa could see a picture of George Washington in their homeroom. I hope this practice will spread so that the "Father of Our Country" will be back in the classrooms, where he should be.

Epilogue

First, I would like to recall that whether as a refugee who lost his parents and his native country, a WWII veteran who lost his leg, or a retired educator who recently lost his wife, increasingly I discovered that the *Horizons of Hope* lie deep in each individual.

There is a Force, some of us call God, that can work through one's innermost soul and can help us to find a new direction and a New Hope for the future.

As more and more people participate in this exciting venture, bitterness and hatred are replaced by love and understanding. Disunity and division are replaced by unity and peace. Broken relationships are healed, restlessness and lack of purpose are superseded by faith and hope, and a New World is slowly emerging.

When I came to America in 1941, I never realized how much it meant to be a free man. Human liberty was something more than I had imagined. Liberty has been the very soul of Czechoslovakia. We knew it, we lived it, yet we only grasped the beauty and greatness on March 15, 1939, when Germany invaded Czechoslovakia, taking away our freedom.

In America, freedom of expression gives creativity. People can grow into well-rounded personalities. In a dictatorship people's lives are filled with fears. People grow numb inside and the top priority of life becomes <u>survival</u>.

Freedom of choice is part of our life here. We have the right to vote, but have become so spoiled by this privilege that in the 2000 presidential elections only half of the voting population actually cast their ballots.

Americans take for granted, which has been theirs for 200 years, but for a refugee, the freedom and liberties here in this country are almost unbelievable. And after all these years, they are just as beautiful to me today, as that day when I first arrived in New York on an overcrowded freighter.

Today the world is invaded by much hope. Sometimes we tend to forget the depression, WWII and the Cold War. Russia is free to make choices about its future, China is showing great promise in developing a new economy, and the danger of nuclear war is receding. Hopefully this trend will prevail, and if it does, the challenge ahead of us is even clearer than before.

Will we listen to the 'still small voice' so often buried, and thus release the moral and spiritual powers that could enable us to deal with the many other problems in need of solutions, and create a world where everyone, rich or poor, black, yellow or white could fulfill his true destiny . . .

Appendix

Dear John,

Germany is united. After four decades of separation, the people in East Germany have become free, in a peaceful and democratic process, without violence and bloodshed. On the basis of free negotiations and of consent with the victor powers of World War II and with our neighbors.

We are breathless and grateful—grateful to God and to many people who worked for reconciliation, for grassroots change and international transformation, for global perspective and new leadership on many levels.

You came to Germany in the very early years after the war. You shared with us hardships and insecurities. You helped to turn desperation and resignation into faith and active responsibility. You built friendships, personally and in national dimensions. You helped to lay a foundation of confidence in a democratic way of organizing society and international relations.

Today, as Germans we want to thank you most warmly for what you did for our country.

The process of freedom and unification only became possible because of the broad foundations that had been laid in the decades before. We think with gratitude of the vital contribution you made and for your comradeship.

We hope that you are well and that some day we can meet and thank you personally. Today we send you our warmest greetings.

In the name of many . . .

Fromund and Konle
Lauzjog and Ruth

Ernd and Marianne
Willi and Barbara

Friendships Renewed at Anniversary

By Tracy Souter - World Staff Writer

Four days of renewing old friendships was how one Tulsan described the silver anniversary of *Up With People* held in Denver recently.

"I have kept in touch with old students over the years, but there were at least 100 people I haven't seen in twenty years," said John G. Pribram, a former vice principal and social studies teacher for *Up With People.*

Up With People, a year long, cross-cultural traveling experience for young adults between the ages eighteen and twenty-six is designed to bring unity between countries through song and dance.

Pribram said that during his association with *Up With People*, from 1966 to 1971, high school students joined the programs.

He said twelve faculty members taught 100 to 150 students the same courses they would normally be taking at home.

Pribram said what made attending the anniversary so special was that it was the first time young adults from the Soviet Union were allowed to travel with Up With People.

More than 3,000 alumni from 25 foreign countries and all-50 states attended the anniversary, Pribram said.

"It was like a huge family reunion," he said. "No, it was more like a world family reunion."

Pribram said that philosophy has carried the students he once taught into adulthood.

"Some have been fighting the environment, the drug problem, some became educators, and others are in the business community," he said. "And they're all concerned about the future."

Pribram said in 1969 a girl from Florida, who was joining the program, had never seen or associated with a black person before.

"While on the trip she met blacks and overcame the deep prejudice she had been taught," he said, "And she discovered that there is no real difference between races."

The White House
WASHINGTON
March 12, 1990

Dear Students,

I was pleased to learn of your support for our nation's war on drugs. By recognizing the dangers of illegal drugs and by taking steps to inform others, you have become an important part of the effort to achieve a drug-free America.

I am heartened by your commitment. You will set a positive example for those around you by remaining drug-free.

Mrs. Bush joins me in sending our very best wishes.

God bless you.

Sincerely,

Gg Bush

Students of Mr. Pribram's
Advanced Civics Class
Union Junior High School
7616 South Garnett Road
Tulsa, Oklahoma 74133

TO: Ken Hancock

FROM: Larry Elliott

DATE: February 19, 1990

RE: John Pribram, Educator of the Month

Union Junior High proudly presents John Pribram as the March Educator for Union Public Schools. Mr. Pribram creates a world of living civics for his students. This teacher, patriot, and refugee personally relates to freedom as he escaped Czechoslovakia just prior to WWII. He then joined the U.S. Army and received the Silver Star on the battlefield for all the rights that democracy represents. Inside his classroom one will find the judicial, legislative, and executive branches being brought into the reality of today's world.

John Pribram is one of those exemplary teachers who demonstrated the relevancy of history to the Twentieth and Twenty-First Centuries. He challenges and nurtures his students by continually inviting prominent guest speakers to relate current events to students' lives in a very meaningful fashion.

Activities outside the classroom give Mr. Pribram other opportunities to impact education. This Harvard University graduate sponsors the National Junior Honor Society, and he is becoming a renowned author and interpreter of European history. His book *Horizons of Hope* will be published soon. His views are often sought by the local media.

Mr. Pribram has been a teacher at the junior high for six years and is definitely a credit and asset to the entire faculty and staff of Union Public Schools.

Thank you, Mr. Pribram, for your contribution to educating our Union students.

Lawmakers in Action
By Keith Edwards

The lawmakers in John Pribram's third hour class discovered what it is like to be in Congress. Each of the students authored a bill about a national issue. Then the students decided in committees whether or not the bill would be sent to the "General Assembly." The students used congressional etiquette in debating each bill.

The president of the session was Erin Acrea. "We discovered that the process of making a bill into a law is much more difficult that it seems," he said, "The lawmaking process takes a long time due to different opinions and views."

The bills that were passed dealt with everything from the environment to abortion. A favorite was a proposal for a four day school week. Jodi Fowler, author of this bill, set it up so that school would have the same number of hours but not as many days.

Students learned a lot about lawmakers. The class will most likely make them more patient with congressmen later in life.

The Communicator, March 1991

Re-enactment of a Supreme Court Case
By Keith Edwards

On September 26, Mr. Pribram's third hour advanced Civics class re-enacted the 1969 Supreme Court case of Tinker vs. Des Moines Independent School District.

In December of 1965, seven students of Des Moines, Iowa decided to protest the Vietnam War by wearing black armbands.

On December 17, the children were called into the principal's office. They were asked to remove the bands to stop some disruption that was being caused. When the students refused, they were suspended from school until they took the bands off.

John F. Tinker and Mary Beth Tinker were two of the five students suspended. Mr. Tinker files a lawsuit against the school. The case of Tinker vs. Des

Moines Schools reached the Supreme Court four years later. The Supreme Court ruled in the students favor, thus protecting the right to protest from the first amendment.

The students Supreme Court ruled in favor of the students with a 7 to 2 vote. The majority felt as if the right to protest shouldn't be limited if there is no clear and present danger of the actions.

The class audience voted 6 to 7 in favor of the students. The students' lawyers were Robin Hearld and Erin Acrea. The school's lawyers were Craig Buchan and Carmen Bingaman. The Justices were Riki Cartwright, Keith Edwards, Jodi Fowler, Jill Wahouske, Joshua Shelton, Josh Risner, James Shimer, and Steven Cianci. The Chief Justice was the Honorable Erin Rusley.

The case gave the class a chance to learn what it is like to be a Supreme Court Justice. This mock trial proved that the students of Union truly value the first amendment rights that they have been given.

The students also displayed that not only adults have political views and convictions. They've shown that we have the talent to make UJH the junior high of some famous political characters. Good work.

PTA NEWSLETTER

An Unusually Exciting Civics Course
John G. Pribram, Social Studies Instructor
Union Junior High School

What do you expect to do in the year 2010? What kind of world do you expect to live in? Those two questions were answered by the incoming eighth grade civics students. The answers revealed a young generation filled with high hopes and high expectations for the future.

When President Bush gave his speech on "Drugs," the students listened with great interest and responded by writing a letter to the president. They committed themselves to a drug-free class and to help those in need of help. They were thrilled to receive a thank you letter from the President. He appreciated their commitment and supported them wholeheartedly.

When we were comparing dictatorship with democracy, a TV channel taped segments of our class activities and the students could see themselves on the evening news.

The tumbling down of the "Berlin Wall" as well as the courageous revolution by Vaclav Havel in Czechoslovakia were followed by the students and their teacher, a native of Czechoslovakia, with utmost interest.

Our Congressman Jim Inhofe spent a whole hour with the students answering questions about our government and the issues we face in the world.

A state senator talked to the students at a time when the most innovative Education Reform Bill was debated in the legislature. The students did not have school for one week, while the teachers went on strike, pressuring successfully the Legislature to implement the much-needed reforms.

There were elections in Tulsa. The city was changing from a commissioner type city government to a mayor council government. Many students had the opportunity to listen to the newly elected Mayor Rodger Randle, who was the guest speaker at the National Junior Honor Society Induction ceremony at our school.

Earth Day and the city problems about the environment inspired the students to write to the mayor. Again they were thrilled to get a thoughtful reply. They discovered that a citizen, old or young, can be heard and can make a difference!

Project Business, Mock Trials, and an in-depth study of our Constitution were other elements of this course.

OCCS Bulletin, March 1991
Oklahoma Council for Social StudieS

World War II
Veteran Finds Peace In Faith

John G. Pribram, who as a teen escaped from Nazi rule in Europe and became an American citizen and soldier, found himself after World War II in Germany counseling Germans about their experiences during the war.

Contributed Photo

Through the Tears
Nora K. Froeschle
World Staff Writer
May 24, 2000

John G. Pribram, 76, still reeling from the bizarre accident that killed his wife in February, is putting on his Purple Heart and a brave face this Memorial Day.

As reported in the Tulsa World on February 24, 2000, Agnete Pribram, 70, died when a car driven by a 92-year-old woman crashed through the front doors of a drugstore at 31st Street and Harvard Avenue, pinning her underneath. She was pronounced dead at the scene.

"Everybody has heard of it," Pribram said. "People say 'oh, you're the one...'" After the accident, Pribram said he received at least 400 condolence messages from here and abroad. He is putting together a book about his wife, which he plans to send to everyone who sent him a sympathy message.

"As a thank you for all of those who supported me," Pribram said.

Pribram met Agnete in 1966 while they were both traveling and working with the *Up With People* organization in Germany.

He helped create the traveling high school where *Up With People's* young performers studied during the day in whatever space, in whatever church, in whatever town they found themselves in.

In the evenings, the teens performed the musical programs for which

Up With People has been recognized around the world.

His marriage proposal was almost as much a shock to him as it must have been to her.

"Then one morning in a quiet time, it came to me to ask the nurse traveling with us to marry me," Pribram said.

The two weren't even dating, but she said yes, which Pribram says he knew she would, and they were soon married in Copenhagen, Denmark.

"Only then as we got to know each other I found that her dad was in the Danish resistance . . . she had similar experiences as me" he said.

Pribram's experiences during World War II sound like the plot of a movie, but instead were lived in tense reality.

In 1938, just before the Nazi rolled into Prague, Pribram left his native Czechoslovakia and went to live with an uncle in Belgium, a neutral country.

Contributed photo Pribram and his late wife, Agnete, took time during the holidays to share one of many smiles.

Community World staff photo
by Nora K. Froeschle

Pribram, 16 at the time, attended school there and was eventually joined by his parents.

Although they were not Jewish, Pribram's parents feared the Nazis greatly as did everyone, he said. They had seen many, many of their friends arrested and sent away to camps.

But, Hitler's soldiers were soon invading Belgium too.

"I woke up at 5 a.m. with planes in the sky and bombs dropping . . . five days later the government asked all young men to leave as quickly as possible to maybe return and fight the Germans later," Pribram said.

He escaped to France on a bicycle.

His parents stayed a little while longer in Belgium and made arrangements to meet up with him in the United States as soon as they could all reach Washington, D.C. at the home of his uncle Karl.

But, Pribram was to learn later that his parents drowned in a river while trying to escape.

"Somehow God looked after me," he said.

While in a refugee camp in France, Pribram caught the attention of a minister who invited him to lunch, then introduced him to a French family who ended up taking him in to live with them for a year. It was there he received the shattering news of his parent's death.

"God's timing was unbelievable—to give me a home and only then let me find out," he said.

In 1941, after a year with his French family, Pribram traveled from France to Spain to meet an uncle with whom he crossed the Atlantic on a harrowing 40-day ocean journey to the United States.

The freighter the two had sailed on was torpedoed and sunk by a German submarine on its return to Europe, he said.

Once in the United States, he enrolled at American University—and promptly met Eleanor Roosevelt.

"One day you are a poor little refugee, and a few months later you meet the First Lady," he said of the twist of fate that put him in a handshake with Mrs. Roosevelt.

She had invited a number of foreign students to tea and he was among them, Pribram said.

Along with being a student, Pribram worked to get himself into the Army.

"I thought 'This is my war as much as anyone else's," he said.

In 1944 in Jackson, Miss., Pribram became a United States citizen and then a combat medic with the Army. They had trained for the Pacific, but were sent to "cold Europe," he said.

"But this was exciting to me. I was to become a liberator in the same places I was a refugee."

His platoon got into combat in a region of France called the Alsace Lorraine.

"There, we were asked to take a hill, and to get to that hill, we had to go through a field," he said. It turned out to be a minefield. "Then, they opened every kind of fire on us and, of course, some of my men were stepping on mines and were wounded. I could hear screams."

Walking in the direction of those screams, Pribram himself stepped on a mine. It took off his right leg below the knee. For his valor, he was awarded the Silver Star and his French family came to see him while he was in the hospital there.

Back in the States in a hospital in Richmond, Va., Pribram learned how to walk again.

Discouraged and depressed, Pribram said a chance visit from some young Christian singers was the catalyst for a change which affected his whole life.

"They told me that 'God has a plan for you and he speaks to you through your conscience . . . it was too much, but then I tried to walk and it didn't work at all. I thought about what those young people told me. They said to take paper and pen and write everything and maybe God will speak to you."

"First I wrote, that the nurses don't know what they're doing and, the doctors don't know what they are doing . . . it was two pages of blame, but then it turned around and I realized I had so much to be grateful for . . . I decided to have faith—to trust God. The next day I could walk."

After finishing his bachelor's degree at Harvard University, Pribram was invited on what he said was "the big one."

"I was invited by friends to participate in a moral and spiritual reconstruction of Europe," he said, adding that at first he did not want to go.

"I was filled with bitterness and hatred. the Germans took my parents, my leg . . . why would I want to go there?" he said. But then he said he was suddenly filled with acceptance. He would spend the next fifteen years in Germany counseling Germans about their war experiences.

Then came Agnete, their marriage and their eventual move to Tulsa in 1971, where they bought the first home either one of them had lived in since childhood.

Pribram taught Social Studies at Monte Cassino School for twelve years and in the Union district for eight, and Agnete worked for a university social science research center.

In their retirement years, she pursued her passionafe hobby—photography—and Pribram wrote his autobiography.

Losing his wife the way he did at this stage of his life seems unbearably cruel, but even in this, Pribram finds hope.

"Her two wishes were fulfilled," he said. "We sometimes talked of the future and she would say 'wouldn't it be nice if we died together in a crash?' and she also said 'I really don't want to get very old.'"

Still grieving, Pribram has no anger at the driver of the car that hit his wife.

"For her it must be pretty tough. You're ninety-two and you kill someone, and you have to live with that."

Pribram tries to keep busy and fill the days he used to spend with Agnete. He visits schools and runs the Military Order of the Purple Heart high school essay contest every year. He also continues to be a volunteer mediator for the County Courthouse.

No stranger to loss, Pribram is moving on with one fervent hope for the future.

"I firmly believe she is in heaven and one day I expect to join her."

Index